The First Part of My Life

by Fannie Brenner

A Publication of JewishGen
Edmond J. Safra Plaza, 36 Battery Place, New York, NY 10280
646.494.2972 | info@JewishGen.org | www.jewishgen.org

JewishGen is the Genealogical Research Division of the Museum of Jewish Heritage – A Living Memorial to the Holocaust

The First Part of My Life

Copyright © 2024 by Rivka Chaya Schiller. All rights reserved.
Published by JewishGen
First Printing: November 2025, Cheshvan 5785

Author: Fannie Brenner
Translated by: Rivka Chaya Schiller

Cover Design: Rachel Kolokoff Hopper

This book may not be reproduced, in whole or in part, including illustrations in any form (beyond that copying permitted by Sections 107 and 108 of the U.S. Copyright Law and except by reviewers for public press), without written permission from the copyright holder.

JewishGen is not responsible for inaccuracies or omissions in the original work and makes no representations regarding its accuracy.

Library of Congress Control Number (LCCN): 2024949997

ISBN: 978-1-962054-12-6 (softcover: 200 pages, alk. paper)

About JewishGen.org

JewishGen, is a Genealogical Research Division of the Museum of Jewish Heritage - A Living Memorial to the Holocaust, serves as the global home for Jewish genealogy.

Featuring unparalleled access to 30+ million records, it offers unique search tools, along with opportunities for researchers to connect with others who share similar interests. Award winning resources such as the Family Finder, Discussion Groups, and ViewMate, are relied upon by thousands each day.

In addition, JewishGen's extensive informational, educational and historical offerings, such as the Jewish Communities Database, Yizkor Book translations, InfoFiles, Family Tree of the Jewish People, and KehilaLinks, provide critical insights, first-hand accounts, and context about Jewish communal and familial life throughout the world.

Offered as a free resource, JewishGen.org has facilitated thousands of family connections and success stories, and is currently engaged in an intensive expansion effort that will bring many more records, tools, and resources to its collections.

Please visit https://www.jewishgen.org/ to learn more.

Vice President for JewishGen: Avraham Groll

About JewishGen Press

JewishGen Press (formerly the Yizkor Books-in-Print Project) is the publishing division of JewishGen.org, and provides a venue for the publication of non-fiction books pertaining to Jewish genealogy, history, culture, and heritage.

In addition to the Yizkor Book category, publications in the Other Non-Fiction category include Shoah memoirs and research, genealogical research, collections of genealogical and historical materials, biographies, diaries and letters, studies of Jewish experience and cultural life in the past, academic theses, and other books of interest to the Jewish community.

Please visit https://www.jewishgen.org/Yizkor/ybip.html to learn more.

Director of JewishGen Press: Joel Alpert
Managing Editor - Jessica Feinstein
Publications Manager - Susan Rosin

Cover Photo Credits

Cover designed by Rachel Kolokoff Hopper

Front Cover:
Fannie Brenner courtesy of Shelly Brenner and family.

Front and Back Cover: background photo and texture, *Dried Grasses in Winter*, Rachel Kolokoff Hopper.

Back Cover:
    Top Left: *Fannie Brenner and her husband* Fredek courtesy of Shelly Brenner and family.
    Top Right: *The young parents, Elye-Motye and Vichne Bokstein with the authoress* courtesy of Shelly Brenner and family. Page 29.
    Bottom Right: *the authoress with her husband and son, Shloymele* courtesy of Shelly Brenner and family. Page 170.

The First Part of My Life

Fannie Brenner

Translated by Rivka Chaya Schiller

For my sons
Shlomo and Benny –
With love

Contents

Dedication	4
Translator's Note	6
Introductory Word – Dr. Y. Ch. Biletzky	10
My Hometown	15
Our Home	25
At the Yiddish School	34
Sweet Childhood Years	40
Cultural Life in Bereza	46
In Bialystok	54
The Second World War Breaks Out	65
Under Soviet Conditions	72
War	79
In Leningrad and Across Russia	85
In Samarkand	94
Resumed Studies	101
Vacation and Further Study	109
Jewish Youths from Poland in Samarkand	115
I Get Married	124
In Lemberg	133
Back on Polish Soil	144
I Become a Mother	155
In Wroclaw	163
For Israel!	172
Index	178

Dedication

The fond memories of my grandmother, Savta Fania started when I was very young. Every summer since I was a baby, my mother Z"L took my brother and me on the long trip, from Toronto, Canada to Israel to visit my paternal and maternal grandparents who lived only a short walk from each other. While the trip was very long and I would endure horrible bouts of air sickness, I loved my summer trips to Israel. I enjoyed the time I spent with Savta. I remember how affectionate and loving she was and always feeding us delicious food, including ktzitzot, a favorite of my brother and mine.

Savta enjoyed caring for my brother and me during those summers. She was protective and would always wave as she watched from her balcony as we would walk to and from our other grandparents' home. The last summer that I saw my grandmother before she passed away, I was only 13 years old. It was only decades later that I realized what a gift she had left for me, my brother, his three sons and my son, and generations to come.

In 2013 my mom Z"L had a recollection that my grandmother had written a book about her early life but it was in Yiddish. My mother, whose career had focused on Holocaust Studies, suggested that I consider getting the book translated into English to learn about my grandmother's life during the war. We found a translator and the book was fully translated in 2014 by Rivka Schiller. The book allowed me a glimpse into my grandmother's life and to better understand what Jewish people endured in Eastern Europe pre-WWII, during WWII and after the war.

Fast forward to 2024, when Rivka approached me about publishing the book in English, I decided to re-read the book again over 10 years later. One key difference is that I am now a mother and have a young son of my own. While re-reading her book, it struck me that the decisions she and her family made changed the trajectory of her life and meant the difference between life and death and will forever have an impact on our family and our future generations. Writing her memoir allows my family's future generations to learn about what our grandmother and her family endured, and this is so precious, as many times stories are passed onto generations through word of mouth and the details can naturally change over time. This gift from my grandmother is that the words in the book will be there unchanged for eternity.

Shelly Brenner, granddaughter of the author

Translator's Note

My introduction to Fannie Brenner's autobiography dates back to at least a decade ago, when I was first contacted by one of the late author's grandchildren about translating *Di ershte helft lebn* [The First Part of My Life] for her family. I was glad to undertake the translation assignment, as the book looked compelling. My main association with Ms. Brenner's town of origin, Bereza Kartuska, prior to reading her account, was that it was the site of the notorious prison established by Polish authorities in 1934 for radical political organizations—particularly Communists. Many left-wing Polish Jews were incarcerated there prior to World War II under harsh conditions for various periods of time. I also appreciated the fact that a woman authored this book, something that one should not necessarily take for granted when it comes to a Yiddish language monograph.

Of additional interest to me was the fact that while Ms. Brenner (1923-1993) and her family resided in postwar Communist Poland, they were active in the relatively small Jewish community that was found primarily in the newly annexed "Recovered Territories" from Germany in the wake of the Second World War. Indeed, Ms. Brenner even taught Yiddish and other subject matter in a Jewish school there. But ultimately, although she and her husband were well-educated and had good professional positions, the reality of persistent antisemitism and the absence of vibrant prewar Jewish life, was definitely not lost on them. Incidents such as their young son being picked on by fellow Polish peers and singled out for being a "Żyd" continued to take on greater significance and perhaps foreshadowed worse times ahead.

As a result, the Brenner family, which grew to four members, ultimately made the weighty and consequential decision to leave their Polish homeland for the Jewish homeland of Israel. Ms. Brenner's parents and brother had already immigrated to Israel in 1950, thereby acting as an additional catalyst in the Brenner family's decision to immigrate to the fledgling Jewish state. After many attempts, Gomułka's government finally permitted the family to leave Poland at the end of 1956. This was the beginning of what Polish historian, Dariusz Stola, refers to as the "Gomułka aliyah." Between 1956 and 1960 close to 51,000 Polish residents obtained emigration permits to Israel.[1]

Subsequently, this wave of Polish Jewish emigration would be renewed in 1967-1968 shortly following Israel's Six Day War of June 1967. It was then that Poland's Jews were publicly accused of being a "fifth column" with misplaced loyalties. A virtual anti-Jewish witch hunt ensued throughout the country during which Jews were singled out and forced out of their jobs—often times, high ranking government positions. This led to an emigration between 1968 and 1970 of nearly 13,000 Polish residents who ostensibly declared Israel their destination point.[2] Ironically, though, unlike the emigration wave during which Fannie Brenner and her family exited Poland for Israel, this later emigration wave witnessed fewer Polish Jews relocating to the Jewish Homeland. Since this autobiographical account only pertains to the "first part" of Fannie Brenner's life, I hesitate to comment too much on her later years, which were spent in Israel. I do know, though, via the memorial book: *Kartuz-Berezeh: Sefer Zikaron Ve-Edut Li-Kehilah She-Hushmedah, H.Y.D.* [Kartuz-Bereza: Memorial Book and Testament to the Community That was Destroyed, May God Avenge Its Blood] (1993), that "Tzipora" Brenner (Tzipora was the Hebrew given name by which Fannie was known) was an active member of the Irgun Yots'e Kartuz-Berezeh be-Erets Yisra'el [the Organization of Kartuz-Bereza Emigrants in Israel] and an integral part of the committee that ultimately published the aforementioned memorial book. Sadly, Ms. Brenner did not live

---

[1] Darius Stola, "Jewish Emigration from Communist Poland: The Decline of Polish Jewry in the Aftermath of the Holocaust," *East European Jewish Affairs* 47: 2-3 (2017): 175-179.

[2] Stola, "Jewish Emigration from Communist Poland," 180.

to see the actual publication of this work. However, her photo, name, and essays—extracted and translated from her Yiddish language memoir—are all featured in this printed testament to a Jewish community that once existed.

As a disclaimer about my choice of transliterated human and place names, I admit to a lack of consistency throughout my English translation of Ms. Brenner's first-person account. To a certain degree, I employed the YIVO system of orthography when encountering Jewish given names and surnames. However, if I happened to know that a given name or surname was spelled a particular way, I made a point of employing the accepted spelling or transliteration of that given name or surname.

In the case of place names, one should bear in mind that Ms. Brenner employed the names that were used during the time when she resided in or near these various places. Thus, for example, she refers to her then Polish hometown as Kartuz-Bereza, Bereza-Kartuska, or simply, Bereza. Yet today, this region is part of Belarus and is presently known as Byaroza. This type of information may be especially significant for individuals who are interested in utilizing Ms. Brenner's memoir (in English translation) for genealogical purposes.

It is also important to mention that the place names Ms. Brenner mentioned throughout her book are frequently the Yiddish versions of these place names. Thus, I have tried to preserve Ms. Brenner's choice of place names, while also adding in parentheses the more universally recognized versions of these names. In certain instances where a small site on the map is mentioned and I was unable to pinpoint the more widely accepted name version, I simply transliterated the place name phonetically per Ms. Brenner's own usage. In light of these discrepancies, I strongly recommend that readers consult the original Yiddish text, if at all possible, as well as a world atlas. This should help to provide additional visual context for the myriad sites in which Ms. Brenner resided—namely, during the first part of her life.

Rivka Schiller, PhD

Introductory Word

The migration of a Jewish woman during the Holocaust period. Believe me, from Kartuz-Bereza to Samarkand is quite a journey! She sought a home in Poland following the Holocaust. Ten years in Poland, a migration, while everything burned, and in each place, she sat on the packages of beans,[3] because the following day she would need to journey further.

The book of a woman who does not flee from herself; rather, the opposite: she is constantly fleeing toward her Jewish self-respect, toward all the values of her home; she only flees from the German bullets and the Soviet Garden of Eden.

A book that does not whisper, does not make a great deal of noise, but relates how an experienced storyteller fled from the Nazi terrorist, where the black pepper grows [i.e., at the end of the world].

An important witness to the Holocaust-picture of a Jewish town.

In principle, the Jewish town everywhere was one and the same – both in Lithuania and in Poland. It was a traditional way of life that spanned generations. Contained within itself and indeed, bound to all that surrounded it, with all the Gentile villages, with all the fields and woods.

Here, Jewish life pulsated strongly, with much energy, with the ups and downs, with a yearning for that which is more beautiful, better, further.

---

[3] This appears to be a figurative expression connoting that the author was in a rather unstable position and that soon enough, she would have to be on the move, once again.

Read the chapter in the book, "Youth in Kartuz-Bereza," and you will see Kadya Molodowsky's "A House with Seven Windows"[4] in her town of birth.

When a Jew would go to Warsaw, he would ride through ten scores of Jewish towns. From the distance, one could see a lit-up religious house of study in which a diligent Talmud student learned at night and forged the golden chain of Jewish life. It was not like this during the Holocaust period – other ways, other eyes, and another heart, which beat with fear and terror.

The book of a woman who saw and heard, and like a turbulent stream, there beat within her the will to live, the "desire of life" to arrive somewhere, where she would be able to live, breathe, study, attain.

A juicy Yiddish. The language buzzes like a beehive.

This book looks sharply at the surroundings. And therefore, these pages are an important document for our Holocaust period. One should read this book and breathe in with all of one's senses the struggle of a Jewish woman treading along the Holocaust's paths. The Vale of Tears of our life, where blood runs like rivers and tears flow like oceans; these were the attendants, lying in these pages.

Temptations and actions and the urge to live – that is the sort of material about which this book relates.

Dr. Y. Ch. Biletzky

---

[4] An English translation of "A House with Seven Windows" and other short stories written by Kadya Molodowsky may be read at the following link:
https://archive.org/details/housewithsevenwi0000molo (accessed 4-13-24).

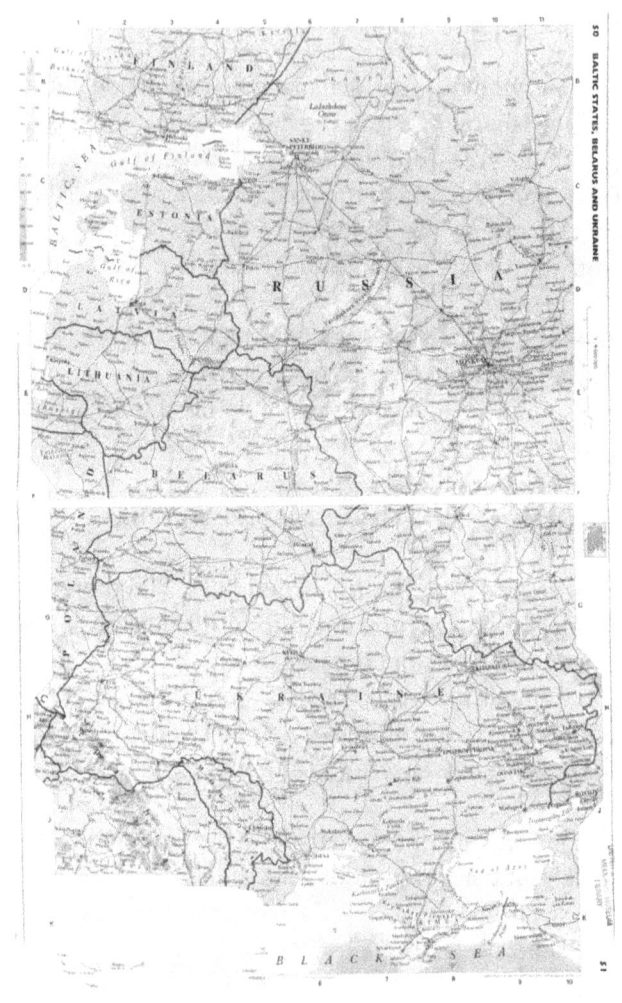

Map depicting Bereza, circled at F3.[5]

---

[5] See: *Oxford Atlas of the World* (New York: Oxford University Press, 1995), 50-51.

Street scene #2 of Bereza-Kartuska, c2015, submitted by Tomasz Wiśniewski to One-Step Webpages by Stephen P. Morse website[6]

---

[6] See: https://www.stevemorse.org/bereza-and-antopol/tomek4.jpg (accessed 6-25-24).

House in Bereza-Kartuska in early 20th century, submitted by Juri Kuvanov from Bereza to One-Step Webpages by Stephen P. Morse website[7]

---

[7] See: https://www.stevemorse.org/bereza-and-antopol/photo057.jpg (accessed 6-25-24).

My Hometown

Summertime. As a bunch of children, we would often go for a walk among the ruins of the old fortress – the monastery of the people of Kartuz – going for walks and searching for treasures beneath the stones that were surrounded by overgrowth and weeds and moss that covered the broken bricks. Every discovery of a sparkling little stone or a piece of colored glass appeared to us like a jewel...

In the winter evenings, Chanukah time, in the hot, heated house, one plucked feathers and fried schmaltz [i.e., chicken or goose fat] and the cracklings of stuffed geese. There, we children would listen to various stories regarding the monastery of the "Holy Brothers" – the monks of Kartuz who built the monastery in the 17th century, during the period of Prince Sapieha. The monastery was likewise a fortress with a watchtower and was surrounded by high walls. The walls of the monastery on the inside – were covered with ground marble. On the floors – pretty, multi-colored mosaic ornaments. Gorgeous furniture, gorgeous pictures on the walls. The monks had gorgeous dishes and eating utensils, and regarding their treasures – gold, diamonds, gems – many legends circulated.

When the weather was nice, we would search for the remnants of those treasures....

At night, however, we were afraid to go near the monastery ruins, because after disturbing the monastery, ghosts and spirits would settle in among the ruins. In the darkness of night, they would crawl out of their hiding places, force their way into Jewish houses; particularly, though, into the horse stalls, and they would drive the horses into a demonic dance.... This is how the town wagon drivers related it.

חורבות פון מאָנאַסטיר ,,קאַרטוזן־ברידער"

Pictures: Ruins of the monastery of the "Kartuz Brothers" (from original Yiddish text and contemporary day photograph)[8]

---

[8] "Ruins of the Carthusian Monastery in Beryoza." For this and other related images of the former monastery from c2023, visit: https://en.belarus.travel/news/ruins-of-the-carthusian-monastery-in-bereza (accessed 6-11-24).

All these tales would accompany us as we moved about, with curiosity, among the ruins of the monastery; however, we would breathe more freely once we had reached the green pastures that surrounded the ruins and had a look around at the pretty surroundings. All around – tall, white-stemmed, shaggy birch trees. And in fact, from all of this – both from the previously functional monastery, as well as from the trees, stems the name of our hometown – Kartuz-Bereza, or Bereza-Kartuska. We, Jews, referred to the town intimately as – Bereza.

My hometown – wooden houses with shingles, only a few double-storied walls, and some ten-score streets; and in the middle – a broad, long street – the road that begins in Warsaw and reaches all the way to Moscow.

Lindens, lilacs, and acacia trees, which grow in the town, fill the air here in the summertime with lively aromas. Old oaks, maple trees, in the autumn, throw off their yellow and red leaves, and to me they look as if they cover the earth with a colorful carpet.

We would have a warm summer in the old hometown. Winter, however, would be cold, with lots of snow and ice. In the in-between period – much rain. It always turned out that we would be stepping in the mud on the unpaved streets. Also, there were the wooden sidewalks, which in the streets, in the middle of town, would be soaked with mud. On a dark evening one had to go out with a lantern, so as not to sink in the mud…. It was only in the 1930s that the arrestees from the concentration camp, which was then established in our town, paved portions of several streets.

And in fact, on account of the concentration camp, our town became infamous in Poland, and even beyond.

Speaking of the concentration camp, one must mention several words about it. In 1934, the anti-Semitic fascist Polish "Sanacja"[9] mimicked its "brothers in thinking" in neighboring Germany, and also established a concentration camp. Transformed were the yet-remaining-from-the-Czarist-period, two or three storied, walled barracks and one smaller wall, near the entrance to the town, where military units had previously been quartered. The large area surrounding this was fenced-off by a three-meter-high fence, with planks, and from both sides – a web of barbed wire. The buildings themselves were once again surrounded by barbed wire. In order to "fully actualize" the model of a concentration camp, prisons were built, which were partially filled with water; and they also established other institutions of torture. An acquaintance of mine who had the "good fortune" of tasting the flavor of this concentration camp, related to me that during the investigations they would torture the arrestee in a horrific manner. They would pour urine into him through his nose. There was much suffering from hunger. Endless military drills on the spot in the worst type of weather. And the forced labor! Here they established a production line of concrete plates to be used to pave the streets and to be placed on the sidewalks. It was difficult to pour this out and to schlep the concrete plates to the places where they had been intended to go. And all of this took place under convoy and with beatings.

The camp existed mainly for Communists, who according to the majority, were punished "administratively," without a trial. No dearth of Jewish boys and girls fell into this place – for distributing Communist leaflets, hanging up red flags on the eve of May 1, or for participating in demonstrations against the Regime. Occasionally, they would also bring gamblers, criminal lawbreakers, here.

---

[9] For further context regarding the Sanacja political movement and the establishment of the Bereza Kartuska concentration camp, see for instance: https://sztetl.org.pl/en/glossary/sanacja (accessed 6-11-24).

We saw them, the camp arrestees, while they were being driven to the work of paving [the streets] in town. The severed, the locked-up ones, with fallen faces... Incidentally, while they were being driven to work, we would have to close the window drapes, so as not to see who had been arrested, and so that one could not communicate with their relatives and acquaintances. Never even mind the fact that it was forbidden to carry on any form of contact with the arrestee. It is no wonder that the word "Kartuz-Bereza" – immediately became an expression – a place where people were demeaned, tortured...

The arrestees were guarded by hundreds of police officers, who were quartered opposite the concentration camp, on the other side of the highway, in houses that had been specially built for them. One said that their number reached five hundred. Also, secret police agents, the so-called "Sniffers," would move about the concentration camp, and from a hidden spot, they would "keep an eye" on the surroundings.

The police officers brought "prosperity" to the town. Tailors, shoemakers had work – they sewed uniforms, upholstered boots. In the shops, buyers appeared, not only on the market days.

The town was poor. The surrounding White Russian villages – even poorer. The peasants used to split a match into four parts. One would joke that every White Russian had his own bus, because on their feet they wore, tied with line rope, rubber slippers, made from old car tires.

In general, the peasants would come to town once a week, on the market day. To purchase something and to sell their products. Whoever from among them had shoes would carry them thrown over their shoulder and would only put them on upon entering a church or a tavern. Their clothing – most of it made from their own woven linen, a sheepskin, a peasant's coat of rough, homespun material, a faded head covering, a worn-out cap on one's head.

In the center of town, in the marketplace, stands with fruit, vegetables, fish. The peasants would bring wagons or sledges with wood to sell in town. In the marketplace stood many rows of little Jewish shops with food products, confectioneries, manufactured goods, metal products, and dishes.

Jews, consisting of five hundred families in our town, constituted more than three-fourths of the population. The remainder – Poles and White Russians. In the Jewish homes and on the street, Yiddish was the leading language. Many Gentiles understood and spoke Yiddish. Shabbat [Saturday] and Sunday the Jewish shops were closed. On Sunday, one would barter one's trade there from behind the scenes.[10]

The locomotive train was somewhat removed from town. One said that the Jews prevailed during the time when it was being built, that the train station, Bludnye,[11] should be located five kilometers from Kartuz-Bereza, so as not to disturb the Sabbath rest...

There were several rather well-off families in town. The rest lived in poverty. There were men who migrated to America in search of a livelihood and left their wives and children behind – literally, at God's salvation – hungry and needy. I remember how on Friday, before Shabbat, I would take a challah and other products

---

[10] This may be an allusion to the fact that Jews were not supposed to be carrying out business on Sunday, the Christian day of rest.

[11] The distance of the Bludnye train-station from Bereza is further substantiated by other works about Bereza. For further information, see for instance: http://stevemorse.org/bereza-and-antopol/ber-hist4.htm (accessed 3-31-24).

to such a needy-suffering family and quietly leave these on their window...

Jews in town were involved in commerce and trade – shopkeepers, tailors, shoemakers, and blacksmiths. There was also an electro-technician, a watchmaker. In the stalls of some of the Jews, cows and goats were kept. Also, a vegetable garden was cultivated. The owners of the dairy products and the vegetables made the situation of a lot of families much easier.

There was almost no construction done in town. Furthermore, it was exceedingly difficult for young couples to find apartments. Married children had to live together with their parents.

Just like in all towns in Poland, Lithuania, and Bessarabia following the First World War, in Kartuz-Bereza a full-blooded Jewish social and cultural life pulsated. Jews always stood out in their awareness for the needs of their fellow Jews and created social establishments to help the needy. In this manner, there existed among us a *Linas-ha-Tsedek*,[12] a charity fund, a cooperative bank; to aid the ill – a hospital, a women's club for social welfare. It is superfluous to convey the significance of these establishments.

Jews were always concerned with their children's education. There was a Tarbut school[13] in Hebrew and a seven-grade school

---

[12] This was a type of charitable organization that tended to the various needs of down-and-out Jews. It was common to find this and similar such institutions in pre-World War II Jewish communities throughout Eastern Europe. There are also institutions with this same name today, generally found among Orthodox or Ultra-Orthodox Jewish communities.

[13] For information about the Tarbut network of Hebrew language, Zionist-oriented Jewish schools that functioned in interwar Poland,

in Yiddish, which were active by us. The youth were active in sports. There was a Jewish library. And it is understood that there were active political groups ranging from the left to the right. There was a Chalutz movement and Beitar.[14] Jews collected money for the Keren-Kayemet[15] and for other Zionist purposes.

The Yiddishist sector, aside from its school, organized a choir, a Lovers' Theater,[16] in which my parents were active in staging performances; they participated in them. Given that I was a student of the Yiddish school, I participated in the theater performances, and sang in the choir.

No less than the worldly, so too, the religious Jews had their own spheres of interest and fulfilled their spiritual needs. Their children learned in cheders [i.e., religious schools for Jewish children prior to high school], in a *Talmud-Toyre* [Torah]. In town, there were several religious houses of study, all built from wood: over and across from the "old" religious house of study – the "new" religious house of study; Tabalitzky's religious house of study; the artisans' religious house of study; opposite it – the Chasidic *shtibl* [i.e., small synagogue]. The Kadisha religious house of study, which was very nicely built, was not too far from

---

see: https://yivoencyclopedia.org/article.aspx/Tarbut (accessed 6-11-24).

[14] Chalutz and Beitar were both Zionist organizations of different ideological bents.

[15] The Keren-Kayemet or Jewish National Fund was founded at the fifth Zionist Congress, in 1901. For further information, visit the organization's website URL: https://www.wzo.il/page/zionist-congress-38/kkl/en a Zionist (accessed 6-11-24).

[16] *Libhobers-Teater* in the original Yiddish. This was apparently the formal name of certain theaters found within different Jewish communities in Eastern Europe, prior to the Second World War.

the marketplace; the religious house of study of the affluent – on "Affluence" Street.[17]

On the holidays, non-religious families who adhered to Jewish traditions would also go to pray.

Although I do not hail from a Chasidic family, it was precisely the Chasidic *shtibl* that drew me in and became etched in my memory. There was an additional reason for this. *Simches-Toyre* [Simchat Torah] would fall out on my and my brother, Berele's, birthday. Our friends would come over to our house and each of them would receive a present – a flag and an apple, which would be placed on the flagstick, and a candle, placed inside of the apple. With the flags in our hands, we would go to the Chasidic *shtibl*, where it was particularly jovial. People sang and danced there. Reb Osher, the father of the currently well-known painter and also poet, Moyshele Bernstein[18] – whose paintings reflect the former Jewish way of life in the small town, as well as its tragic demise – would always outdo himself with his singing and dancing. They not only represent a *kaddish* [i.e., the Jewish prayer for the dead] for our hometown of Bereza, but they are a *kaddish* for all the Jewish communities that were obliterated by the Nazi murderers.

And just like Moyshele Bernstein serenades our hometown in his song, "My Hometown Bereza":

---

[17] This may very well have been a nickname used by local Jews for the street's actual name.

[18] For further information about Bernstein, see for instance: https://www.infocenters.co.il/gfh/notebook_ext.asp?book=155845&lang=eng&site=gfh; https://congressforjewishculture.org/people/5259/Bernshteyn,%20Moyshe%20(August%202015,%201920%E2%80%93December%202006) (accessed 6-22-24).

I am coming to you, my little hometown of Bereza,
When the morning is yet still pale,
Come and listen to my father's Gemara hymn
With the morning song of a bird;
Come and soak up the scent of orchards in bloom...
My memory is awakened to everything –
To the smoke of a chimney,
To the noise of wagon drivers who tighten the reins of horses,
To mothers who pair themselves up, beginning their work in the kitchen,
To the doves that coo upon the rooftops,
To Jews who go early in the morning to the religious house of study
In awe and piety.
To you, Bereza, I come in at a late nighttime hour
When couples go strolling along the path,
To the whisperings of boys and girls
On porches, in the thicket of the trees...
To the muddy alleyways and streets,
To the river and the still tides surrounding the town....
To you, my burnt Bereza, I come.
With yearning and quivering
I sob into my days and nights
Your sob, Bereza...

My love, my unforgettable hometown! A poor, but pretty, honest, morally clean, deeply Jewish way of life pulsated there until September 1939, when Nazi Germany overtook Poland and ignited the terrifying conflagration of the Second World War. In its blaze, six million Jews and the Jewish way of life in Eastern Europe were destroyed.

There was a hometown, there was a Jewish Kartuz-Bereza, there was, and is no more...

Our Home

We lived in the house of my grandfather, my mother's father, Meir-Yossel Zalevsky. It was typical of a small town; it was not a painted wooden house with a porch. There were five rooms, a kitchen, lobby, and a small storehouse or granary whose roof opened up in a corner and was covered with *schach* [i.e., the coverage – frequently from conifer trees – used to create a roof for a sukkah]. We had a sukkah.[19] There was a cellar, an attic beneath the shingles. In the yard – a stall in which to keep firewood for heating the ovens. One – in the middle of the house to heat up all the rooms; the other – in the kitchen, to cook and bake. Behind the stall was a rather large garden – beds for planting vegetables. I loved to help plant the radishes and onions at the sides of the beds, carrots, beets, and cucumbers in the middle of the beds – everything for a singular purpose. From above, we planted potatoes. Cherry and plum trees, the shrubs of gooseberries, raspberries, and currants – near the fence that surrounded the garden.

In the anteroom leading into the house stood a large metal barrel, where Michael the water carrier would pour in the two buckets of water, which he had drawn from the river and carried over with a yoke. There stood, also, a ladder to climb up to the attic, where one dried the laundry and where all the things that had become unnecessary were kept. I used to love climbing up to the attic and resting among the scattered objects there. And how great was my joy when I found a treasure of Yiddish books, mostly plays. At the little rooftop window, I would greedily read them, and would laugh at the comedies, cry at the tragedies and melodramas. Why were these very books being kept in the attic? Of course, on account of the crowdedness in the house. There was no place in which to place another bookshelf.

---

[19] For a definition and the significance of the Hebrew word, sukkah, see for example: https://www.myjewishlearning.com/article/the-sukkah/ (accessed 6-11-24).

In the storehouse or granary and in the cellar stood barrels with fermenting cucumbers and cabbage, pitchers with jams made of strawberries and plums.

In the kitchen, in the large oven, one would bake challah for Shabbat and place the cholent.[20] Under the oven, as was usual, an enclosure. In it – an indentation in which to hold potatoes. To go down over there with a candle, to the grating grates and collect the potatoes in a basket, was for me the worst work.

As I said, this was my grandfather's house. He and my step-grandmother had their own room. On the door, my uncle, my mother's brother, Leizer, engraved: "Madame Krupnik-Varenya." He had returned home from Argentina on account of his difficult diabetes and died at the age of twenty-eight. He did not fit in with his stepmother, who was terribly stingy. In her bed, she would hide eggs in a cap, and in a stocking – oil in a bottle.

Grandpa's daughter, Chaya, and her husband, Dovid Goldberg, fled to Leningrad in the beginning of the 1920s, after the Bolsheviks had been driven out. The Poles arrested him for active Communist operations, during the time that the town was in the hands of the Bolsheviks; and he was sentenced to death.

---

[20] Cholent is a Jewish slow-cooked stew traditionally prepared for the Sabbath or other Jewish holidays.

מײַן זײדנס משפּחה. עס זיצן פֿון (לינקס): די באָבע פֿײגל, דער זון לײזער, דער זײדע מאיר-יאָסל זאַלעװסקי; עס שטײען (פֿון לינקס): דער זון משה, די טאָכטער װיכנע (מוטער פֿון דער אױטאָרין), די טאָכטער חיה (קלאַראַ), איר מאַן דוד גאָלדבערג, דער זון דוד

Photograph: My grandfather's family. Sitting (from the left): Grandma Faigel, their son, Leizer, Grandpa Meir-Yossel Zalevsky; standing (from the left): their son, Moyshe, their daughter, Vichne (mother of the authoress), their daughter Chaya (Clara), and her husband, Dovid Goldberg.

Their son, Dovid, was held in a fortress in Brisk. With his money, Grandpa sold his cow, bribed the prison guards, freed Dovid, and he and his wife managed to cross over the border into Soviet Russia.

Grandpa's eldest son, Dovid, immigrated to America and became an active leader there in the "union" of the hatters [or furriers] in Philadelphia. Grandpa's second son, Moyshe, died tragically while at work at the town mill. He was cranked into a machine's transmission.

In this manner Grandpa's youngest daughter, Vichne – my mother – continued to live with him.

My grandfather – an old Jew with a short grayish little beard and good, smiling eyes. He would sew caps and sell them in his little shop in the marketplace. People called him "The Hatter from Shereshev," due to the fact that he hailed from a small town, Shereshev, next to Pruzhany. He died before my very own eyes from a heart attack. Grandpa returned home one evening very tired, sat down on a large chair next to the large oven, and with pleasure related for those at home, how I had come into his shop and asked him for five groschen to buy a chocolate. However, if he did not have it now, I would come some other time... In the middle of speaking, he suddenly let out a snore, and fell off of the chair, dead.

It is unnecessary to relate the chaos at home. They delivered me to the neighbors, the Resniks, although the children there had the measles. "All at the same time, a child must go through having the sickness" – said their mother.

Following Grandpa's death, my step-grandmother returned to Brisk, from which she hailed, and where she was a teacher.

די יונגע עלטערן עליע־מאָטיע און וויכנע באָקשטיין מיט דער אויטאָרין

Photograph: The young parents, Elye-Motye and Vichne Bokstein with the authoress

Our family, alone, now remained in Grandpa's house – my parents, Vichne and Elye-Motye Bokstein, I, Faigele, and my two little brothers, Berele and Leizerke. My mother took over the inheritance – the house and the shop. The shop did not merely generate a small degree of concern. Many of the customers were workers from the local sawmill, former members of the White Guard,[21] who would purchase everything on loan, with

---

[21] The White Guard or White Army fought against the Bolsheviks following Russia's October Revolution. During the Russian Civil War of 1918-1921, they opposed the Red Army. For further information

promissory notes, and at some point, would disappear. The little shop was left without merchandise, with a pack of unfulfilled promissory notes. My father would fruitlessly search for them, the delinquent payers, in the surrounding area – on a sled, on a bicycle.

At home by us, the hatter, Shayme Kagan, would work sewing caps. While working, he would sing Chasidic songs and tunes. Since then, I have loved cantorial music. I used to love singing. The man who cut my hair, Sapir, would have me sit on a board on top of the haircutting chair, and prior to cutting my hair, he would ask me to sing him a song. Often, I would sing him:

> At my window, in my garden
> Grow all sorts of flowers.
> Then a naughty child came along
> And grabbed the flowers...

And as I am recalling my great desire for singing, my memory is stirred with the people who strengthened this desire within me and brought me contentment.

It turned out that my parents must have been strapped for cash, because they rented out my grandfather's room, first, to the teacher named Shaftan, and his wife; later on, to the teacher named Boyan, his wife, and child. He would sing their child nice little songs, and I would listen in and mimic him:

Oh, my head hurts me.

Inside of my head there is an apple rolling around...

---

about these different movements, see for instance: Richard Pipes, *A Concise History of the Russian Revolution* (First Vintage Books Edition, December 1996).

Not far from us lived the music teacher, Leibel Kaplan. For hours at a time, I would sit beneath his window and listen to the most beautiful opera arias and melodies, which were carried from his gramophone, or entirely from his fiddle.

The teacher, Rochel [Rachel] Chmiel-Shapiro, would play the accordion; and then again, I would listen to the sounds, which were carried from there. Dr. Arian's wife would teach bright children how to play the fiddle, free of charge. My ears also perked up about this.

I used to really like sitting on the floor at the neighbors' house – the shoemaker, Kagan – and listening to his sons, Shayme, Shilim, and Hershel, with their lovely singing and guitar playing. Their sister, Machlye, was my best friend. I could always go to their home and hear the singing and playing of her brothers. Their father, the shoemaker, would sit on a low stool while repairing shoes in his workshop, and accompany his work with tunes. Until this day, I recall the folksong that he loved:

I will bind a stone upon my heart
And I shall throw myself in the *pastovnik*...
That is to say, in the firefighters' water reservoir.

אַ גאַס אין קאַרטוז-בערעזע מיטן פּאַסטאַווניק

Photograph: A street in Kartuz-Bereza with the firefighters' water reservoir

Today, the firefighters' wind instrument orchestra! Their playing at the parades, their repetitions, which I would run to hear! Until today, I recall their repertoire: "A Jewess, a Jewess who died while yet a girl" and "I have a wife, she is sugar-sweet, Chana-Bayla from Paris…"

Friday night by us was chaotic. A small matter – Sabbath eve [Erev Shabbat]! The Yiddish-speaking maid, Nadya, would clean the house, wash the floors, and place doormats on the clean floor. She would also help my mother bake and cook. I was a huge *nosher* and needed to have a taste of the baked goods just after they emerged from the oven. Until today, I [still] taste the flavor of blueberry cake and of those cinnamon cookies. From the cake, I would cut out the middle, the tastiest part. I also did not hold back from getting up on a bench and retrieving the large flask of vishniak [cherry liquor] from the cabinet and having a good sip… Friday evening. We were combed-out and festively dressed, ready to usher in the Sabbath. On the white tablecloth – two candlesticks. My mother would light the Sabbath candles. She would make the blessing… Two covered challahs. The utensils waited at the table. We would eat gefilte fish, broth with noodles, chicken with carrot tzimmes, and compote. We would be happy, and I would kvell, literally melt from pleasure...

Sabbath day, following the cholent and the other foods, my father and mother would take a nap. We children knew that if the weather were nice, they would take a walk outside and take us along with them. In general, we would go to the "lines." That is to say, along the train rails. Conifer trees grew here from both sides of the rails, and we would hear the voices of youths who were being mischievous in the thicket of trees. Here and there in town, one would pass grain fields sprinkled with blue cornflowers. My male and female friends would mimic my parents, the way that they would go arm-in-arm during their walks. I was actually pleased by the way in which my parents conducted themselves. However, I was not angry at my friends for poking fun, and I would laugh along with them.

At the Yiddish School

I recall: I turned five years old, and I was taken from the kindergarten, and was guided to the Yiddish school. I was dressed in my festive pink dress with pleats, wearing new shoes. A pretty pink band in my hair. I was serious, tense. My heart beat more strongly. My eyes gaped, looking with wonder and curiosity at everything.

The school – a single-story, brick-walled building, one of a few brick-walled structures in a positively "wooden" town, as Bereza was. It was no wonder – the area is a wooded one, rich in timber.

I was led into a room: there were rows of long, wooden benches, combined with a table bearing holes in which to place inkwells. For the time being, we did not use any ink. Sharpened pencils and notebooks were distributed to us. It was a fiery moment: we were going to begin learning the alphabet [Alef-Beys]!

Learning took quite a long time (so it seemed to us...). Children grow restless. They cannot sit for too long. But then there was the dismissal – a ringing – the first recess. It was the first in my life as a student. Everyone poured out, as if from a cage, outside. We played pranks in the schoolyard. It was a large, open space. I became acquainted with the students from the class. One did not notice how quickly time passed; and then again, there was a longer, drawn-out ringing, which called us back into class. Once again, I was seated upon the worn bench and listened patiently to the teacher's talk. She won over my heart...

לערערס און טוערס פון דער בערעזער יידישער שול.
עס זיצן (פון רעכטס) די לערערין פעלד, פֿאָרזיצער פון שולראַט שלמה וויַינשטיין, חוה סעגאַל ; עס שטייען (פון רעכטס) : לייבל באיאן, גיטע שאַפטאַן, אליהו שאַפטאַן

Photograph: Teachers and leaders of the Bereza Yiddish school. Sitting (from the right) the teacher, Feld, chairman of the school board, Shloyme Weinstein, Chava Segal; standing (from the right): Leibel Boyan, Gite Shaftan, Eliyahu Shaftan

I remember my teachers up until today. I very much liked the lectures of my teacher, Chana Biltshik, who took us on many walks and drew us closer to nature – to the secrets of growth and blossoming, of tree and plant, animal, and human being. Both inside and outside of class, she taught us to see and understand what and who surrounds us.

I cannot forget the music teacher, Leibel Kaplan, who very successfully led our choir and mandolin orchestra.

I loved the Polish lectures of the teacher, Dr. Rochel Chmiel, and of the photogenic teacher, Feld. I very much liked her long fur coat, and she frequently liked my literary works. It was bound to happen that one particular night a conflagration broke out in town. The entire town ran out to see it – whom indeed to help, and others, simply because they were curious. I, however, slept heavily and slept through the entire conflagration... Not a single thing did I hear or see. Unexpectedly, teacher Feld compensated us with an in-class writing assignment to describe the conflagration. What was I to do? I sat for a long time, in a state of despair, and did not write a single line. Until I took to describing how I imagined this event. When our teacher returned our notebooks, she read my account in front of the entire class as excellent student work. I returned home happy. Not finding my mother at home, I ran to her in the shop, so as to delight her with my success.

I was a bit afraid of the older, stricter teacher, Yoyne [Yona] Resnik, who taught us accounting, although I was also a particularly good student in his class.

It goes without saying that around our teacher, Eliyahu Shaftan, who lived in a room by us, I felt very much at home. (Indeed, he was a familiar person.) He taught us Yiddish.

In the later lectures I particularly liked the lectures about Yiddish literature. I was very much taken with the stories, "Bontshe the Silent" and "If Not Higher" by I. L. Peretz. Sholem Aleichem was remarkably close to my heart. "The Town" by Shalom Asch was less interesting. For children there were too many descriptions. My hometown, our way of life and people, were closer and dearer to me...

As previously mentioned, I loved singing. And among us in town, we would hear singing outside of school wherever we went: in the homes, summer evenings, in the evening – on the floors and porches of the houses, in the woods and fields, while taking a walk. Even while bathing in our river, the Yaselda [Jasiołda, in Polish]... Indeed, it was a poor town, like most of the Jewish towns in Poland and White Russia, but a happy one, one that was content with what it had. Just, as they say in Hebrew, "he who is happy with his portion." There were no thieves, nor criminals among us. As for murderers, it is not even necessary to remark that they did not exist. Crazy people, specifically, did exist...

But let us return to the school. During the long recesses we would run to Malke Gershgorn's little shop to buy a roll and a piece of halvah. That was tastier than the food we had brought from home. But on Fridays all the children would eat at home and in class – potato latkes. The entire town would smell of the latkes and baked puddings that were baked with schmaltz or oil. "Bereza Puddings" was our nickname. As is known, all the Jewish towns literally "had to" have a nickname... Incidentally, children in Bereza would eat this pudding on Yom Kippur, while all the adults and youths, in general, were fasting.

Our gymnastics teacher, Itzel Karolitzky, very much popularized physical culture, and sports. Thanks to him, among us, children, youths, and even adults would do gymnastics. In a room or outside. They would even do gymnastics with bars and rings. They would play in our schoolyard hand and net ball. The muscular fellow, Chaimke Alexandrovsky, would stand out during these games, and many of us were quietly envious of him; whereas we children would sit on the gathered-together boards on top of the building area and watch the games.

The Yiddish seven-year [grade] school in Bereza had a good name throughout the entire area, thanks to its devoted teachers' collective and the high results of its educational-pedagogical work. With that, it placed the local Polish *"powszechny"* [i.e., elementary] school in the shadows. Apparently, on account of this, the Poles, in fact, sought a reason to close this important Jewish institution of learning. One day before the end of the school year in 1934, a commission appeared and decided that the building was not appropriate for a school. There needed to be a longer corridor with doors to every class. The classrooms were too small; they needed to have larger windows. And the outcome – that by the new school year, they would need to rebuild everything; otherwise, they would close the school.

A commotion developed in town. They called together a large public meeting. They selected a building committee to work out a plan to rescue the situation. Indeed, the committee right away established a precise plan as to how and with what means to rebuild the school building. No money was demanded of anybody. They only asked for free labor and building materials for the disposal of this entity. And indeed, this is how it happened. Carpenters made doors and windows. Wagon drivers brought over bricks, quicklime, and sand. Locksmiths accepted the responsibility for assembling the necessary metalware, and they kept their word. The work itself was carried out for free by local craftsmen – bricklayers, carpenters, roof-layers. Adults did the unqualified building work. Children also helped to unload building materials, and cleaned the bricks of the building's walls, which were disassembled, so as to reuse them. With buckets, they presented mortar and sand to the bricklayers and plasterers. It goes without saying that the Jewish housepainters distributed the quicklime and painted all the rooms and corridors, free of charge. The adults often worked until midnight because they would begin working after their normal workday activities.

Everything was complete for the new study year – the school was rebuilt, and two additional classrooms had also been built.

The dedication was turned into a true public holiday. The women prepared nicely covered tables in all the rooms of the building, because they were expecting a huge crowd. The celebratory opening of the building took place in a fully packed large hall. The mood was an exalted one. Lo, what could be achieved with unified efforts! The work had been a successful enterprise just for the sake of angering the antisemites.

Shloymeke Weinstein, who opened the evening, was so overcome that for a long time, he was unable to utter a single word. Tears stood in peoples' eyes.

After the official part, people ate, sang, and danced until early dawn.

When the Polish commission arrived before the beginning of the school year for the inspection, all of its members shrugged their shoulders, literally not wanting to believe their eyes: How had they managed in such a short amount of time to complete such building efforts? Not having any other choice, they signed off on an act – a permit for the school board to begin teaching.

The Jewish population was proud and happy. The school was able to continue the important pedagogical work which it had carried out the entire time; and now it would be able, with greater success, to carry this out further.

Sweet Childhood Years

We were free of school. Summer vacation.

In the morning, an older woman brought the *hulnikes* – hot buckwheat cakes. With a glass of fresh milk from the neighbor's cow, it was the flavor of the Garden of Eden. It was the best breakfast. My father and mother left for the shop. I made up the beds in the bedroom and sang the popular Polish song: "What is a grown-up girl dreaming about, when she turns from a bud into a flower?"

The sun shone in through the window. Luring. I could not miss out on the experience and left behind the housework; and together with my closest girlfriends, Machlye and Mirele, we went down to our river, Yaselda. Alongside the church we guarded ourselves against the priest's large St. Bernard dog. From a small plum tree in a park, we tore off the largest plums. This way, we had sustenance for the road...

We strode through the *"wygon"* – a pasture field for cows – up to the wooden bridge over the Yaselda. On the grass on the left side of the river grazed cows, but the right side served as a beach for the town's youth. Adults would also come here, holding children by the hand.

In a woolen blue bathing suit, an adroit little girl with a smiling face, with dimples in her cheeks, I went swimming, playing with the boys. The good-looking, pleasant-natured little fellow, Vovik Levinson, the son of the town's vice mayor, attached himself to me. Moyshele Bernstein drew my portrait on a box. The group swam the full length of the river, back and forth. I myself learned how to swim. I competed with the swimmers.

The Poles Makiewka and Chorew moved around on the shore with their wagons, selling ice-cream. Having a good time, somebody would take an ice-cream cone and follow the river along to the surrounding villages. There, one would drink cold buttermilk from the black earthen clay jugs and eat pickles.

We would swim past green fields, woods, huts with thatch roofs. The peasants who worked in the fields greeted me with a resounding, "God's help!"

We spent that sun-lit summer day nicely and pleasantly.

At home, a red borsht and meat cutlets awaited me. (Incidentally, the only foods which my mother taught me how to prepare). My mother prepared part of the table, which was covered with a clean tablecloth. My father and both of my brothers were already waiting impatiently for the food, for my arrival. There was a good mood at the table. It turned out that this had been a good day for sales at the store. My mother related how she had pulled out a stolen cap from beneath the skirt of one particular peasant, and also slapped her... And there was also an account about how a woman in the marketplace had placed a stolen fish in her basket. So, the seller removed the fish, saying: "Fish, fish, where have you wandered off to?"

My father was in a rush to get to a meeting at the Yiddish school. They needed to prepare the annual children's performance.

Evening fell. We went outside for a stroll along the avenue. We drank soda water at Resnik's and bought a chocolate biscuit for five groschen. Chaim Alexandrovsky and Taibele Kaplan attached themselves to me and complimented me that I would someday be a pretty girl. Hearing this, it seemed to me that the whole world was mine, and that I would indeed attract Vovik Levinson's attention. And here, he presented himself on the other side of the avenue. I felt a strange weakness in my feet. I pulled the belt around my waist, so that I would appear more nicely shaped. I hastily gulped down the chocolate that I was holding in my mouth and gave him a smile. His good response – a smile – warmed my heart...

וואָוויק לעווינזאָן

Photograph: Vovik Levinson

Vovik approached us and we went for a stroll together. I really wanted to take his hand, but I was embarrassed... Additional friends approached our company. We then became a full gang of girls and boys.

It was a light, warm summer evening. We told each other various stories, which we had read in books and in newspapers, and heard from people. And at this point, we began to sing. The best style, intimate and melting in a high-pitched voice, and all the more strongly and loudly. Our singing woke people from their slumber. One of them, a policeman, ran out of his house in long underwear and screamed at us that we should quiet down. We paid him real heed. But factually, it was already late, and we parted ways, with each of us returning to his or her own home.

Later on, Vovik sent me heartfelt letters from Vilna, where he studied at a technical institute...

One must also add to our children's pranks our picking fruit from foreign orchards. When encountering an orchard, I needed to wear my red underwear with the strong elastic (from the performance "The Hen Strike" by Sholem Aleichem), so that there would be somewhere to hide the apples. On more than one occasion we threw the apples over a fence, to the arrestees in the concentration camp, who worked there.

After such a day, one would return home hungry and throw oneself on the food. We would still play a bit of "under the plate" [i.e., a type of children's game] with nuts and horse chestnuts. And when we went to bed, I would place a small book that I had taken out of the library underneath the pillow, so that the following morning I would be able to read while lying in bed. Following such a day, one falls asleep right away. One sleeps very well.

Autumn was gray and depressing. The skies were always cloudy. It rained a lot. We children lived it up with the coming of winter. We would stomp in the snow, throw snowballs, build snowmen, play pranks, and laugh. What a pleasure! The greatest pleasure was, however, skating across the ice along the river's shore, on the *pastovnik*, on the train rails. On more than one occasion I stood in a burning frost, stomping my feet in my shoes with the red woolen socks, standing and watching how one danced on the ice.

I did not have my own skates. I would go knocking at Dinke Shapiro's and borrow her skates for a couple of hours. While skating, it once happened that I fell with my head on the ice. At Itzel Goberman's house they placed cold compresses on me. However, later on, I once again returned to skate...

At the river, next to Leikele Halpern's house, we used to sled downhill. One time I got caught in a passing sleigh, and the peasant suddenly goaded the horse. Terrified, I barely managed to tear myself free from the sleigh. I was a prankster, and I sought out "adventures."

For us children, the winter had two joyful holidays. Chanukah – playing with dreidels and eating latkes. Purim – with the hamantashen and shalach-mones, and the Purim *shpils* [plays], Purim evenings in the synagogue, with dancing, singing, and good foods. Yet, one still longed for spring, for warmth and sunshine, and waited for the nice springtime day of Lag Ba'Omer.[22] In the morning, we gathered together in the synagogue yard, paired ourselves up, and went out singing across the streets of the town. We would compete with the Hebrew school [i.e., a Jewish school whose focus was on Hebrew], which had a longer column. Mulik Garber led them with the trumpet.

In the woods, several kilometers beyond the town, wagon drivers, the parents of us children, drove us. In the woods, on the grass, we unpacked our food. One tasted the foods that the other had brought. We would play various games, dance, and sing. Our teacher and also several parents accompanied us.

Yes, we waited for springtime impatiently, so that we would be able to go riding on our bicycles. Until I learned how to ride a large bicycle, the frame and saddle would leave behind blue

---

[22] Lag Ba'Omer is a minor Jewish holiday that falls between Passover and Shavuot. For additional information about its significance, see for instance: https://www.myjewishlearning.com/article/lag-baomer/ (accessed 6-11-24).

marks on our thighs and legs. More than once, I fell off of it and banged myself up really well. To this day, I have a hole in one of my knees, on account of a bicycle. However, I learned how to ride well. (Incidentally, thanks to this, I saved my life, while fleeing from the Germans.) On our bicycles, we would ride out to the surrounding woods and pick blueberries. And everything as a group, with a lively racket and mischief…

How true Mordechai Gebirtig's[23] verses sound:

Childhood years, sweet childhood years,
You remain forever awake in my memory.

---

[23] Mordechai Gebirtig (1877-1942) was a Yiddish poet and songwriter, born in Krakow, who was murdered by the Nazis in 1942, while being deported to the Belzec death camp.

Cultural Life in Bereza

Since an early age, I have always loved to read. The books that I would receive as a present were unable to sate my thirst for reading. The town library, where I was registered and borrowed books, helped me out. And already at a rather young age, I literally gulped down works of Yiddish literature and world classics, which were translated into Yiddish. In this manner, aside from the then-popular Shalom Asch, Opatoshu, Segalowitz, I read Rolland, Hamsun, Victor Hugo, Tolstoy, and Gorki. Jules Verne developed fantasy. With him, one swept across the world, in the depths of the sea, and in the air. I also read Polish – Sienkiewicz, Reymont, Mickiewicz, and Orzeszkowa. One time, the librarian recommended a book to me, which she convinced me to read. I pushed it down under my pillow, with the intention of reading it in the morning. This was John Reed's, *Ten Days that Shook the World*. However, I absolutely did not enjoy that book. The history with Kerensky, the overthrowing of the Czar, and the further developments in Russia, did not interest me, being practically yet a child.

In town, there used to be literary evenings, lectures with the participation of guests from Warsaw. And everything in Yiddish. It is understood that this was mainly for adults. My father related to me that the great writer, Peretz Markish, who appeared by us with a lecture, was accompanied by hundreds of people to the train.

The best Yiddish artists used to come to us with their troupes: Zygmunt Turkow, Ida Kaminska, and Diana Blumenfeld. However, when itinerant Yiddishist actors performed *"Chałture"* [Pol. *"Chałtura"* – meaning "hackword" or "potboiler"], people often whistled and threw rotten potatoes at them.

My parents were socially active, particularly in theater matters, and would invite guest role actors to our home, so as to save on expenses. I used to have to give them my room, and I would sleep on the floor in my parents' bedroom. Until... Several itinerant actors stayed over by us and robbed us – they cleaned out my winter clothes closet. And so I rebelled, and we closed the "Actors' Inn"...

Why were my parents so favorable toward Yiddish actors? Quite simple. My father had a strong affinity for social activities. He was the chairman of the Yiddish theater building, and he organized the performances held therein. It goes without saying that he was not paid a single groschen. The only wage – a lot of headaches and worries, which he was also not lacking without this.

The theater – a large wooden building in the yard of the Yiddish school. There was a spacious room with wooden benches, a high stage, and in front of it – a spot for the orchestra. Behind the curtains – a place to keep the decorations [i.e., scenery], a corner for the artists. At the entrance to the room – a buffet.

The traditional annual children's performances at the Yiddish school, which would take place in the theater, were a town attraction. The residents would come in droves. Visitors would even come from the surrounding Jewish settlements. The mood among the crowd was always an exalted one. One would forget one's daily cares and worries.

I would nearly always participate in the performances. I played leading roles in Sholem Aleichem's "Hens' Strike," and in other performances I was the "summer queen," and the "old hamantash." When I did not receive the female role in "Robin Hood," it bothered me greatly.

The parents of the little "artists" would reap joy from their children on the stage. Aside from performing, I would also dance, sing in the choir, and take part in the gymnastics and in the pyramids, which we would form.

The costumes would be prepared before the performances by the parents and teachers. The teachers, Berman and Moyshel[e] Friedman, would paint the decorations [scenery].

Oddly, my parents were indifferent to my "artistic" appearances, although they reaped joy from their daughter. However, they showed me nearly no recognition – seldom gave me a kiss, a caress, praise. I remarked about this, given my parents' preoccupation with the organizational matters concerning the performances, and given their appearances at the local drama circle's spectacles.

I recall how they took part in Sholem Aleichem's "The Great Prize." My mother played Eti-Meni, the tailor Shimele Soroker's wife, who, after having won the large sum of money, took to calling herself Ernestina Yefimovna. The teacher, Chava Segal, played Baylke and sang this heartfelt folksong:

Paper is indeed white, and ink is indeed black,
To you, my sweet life, my heart pulls me...[24]

---

[24] These lines form part of a longer Yiddish song known as "Papir iz dokh vays" ["Paper is Indeed White"]. For additional information about this musical piece, as well as the actual song lyrics, see: https://yiddishsongs.org/papir-lz-dokh-vays-2/ (accessed 6-11-24).

דער דראמאטישער קרייז ביי דער יודישער שול אין בערעזע, אנגעפירט פון שלמה ווינשטיין. עס שטייען (פון לינקס):
אליהו טקאטש, זלאטע ווינשטיין, שילים קאגאן, לייבל באיאן, לייבל פאדאסטרויצע, משהל נאוויק, שלמה קאמע־
נעצקי, הערשל קאגאן, ניטל טקאטש, זינדל קאוואל, יאסל בילטשיק, משהל קאוואל ; מיטלסטע ריי ; הערשל קראניק,
וויכנע באקשטיין, חוה סעגאל, שלמה ווינשטיין, גיטע שאפטאן, זעליק זאקהיים, חייטשע יאלאן (זאקהיים), עליע־
מאטיע באקשטיין, עליע שאפטאן ; פאדערשטע ריי : שייע קאוואל, ביילקע טשעסלער, יאנקל זאקהיים, רחל גארבער,
משהל פרידמאן, רבקה קאוואל, ביילטשע ריסקער, וואווע ווינשטיין

Photograph: The dramatics circle at the Yiddish school in Bereza, run by Shloyme Weinstein. Standing (from the left): Eliyahu Tkatch, Zlata Weinstein, Shilim Kagan, Leibel Boyan, Leibel Podostroytse, Moyshele Novik, Shloyme Kamenetzky, Hershel Kagan, Nittel Tkatch, Zindel Koval, Yossel Biltshik, Moyshele Koval; in the middle row; Hershel Kronik, Vichne Bokstein, Chava Segal, Shloyme Weinstein, Gite Shaftan, Zelik Zackheim, Chayetshe Yalon (Zackheim), Elye-Motye Bokstein, Elye Shaftan, bottom row: Shaye Koval, Baylke Tshesler [Chessler], Yankel Zackheim, Rochel Garber, Moyshele Friedman, Rivka Koval, Bayltshe Risker, Vove Weinstein

The performances were directed by Shloymke Weinstein, Vove's father. The dances were organized by Emma Kaplan; the Polish scenes – the teacher, Chmiel-Shapiro.

The teacher, Leibel Kaplan, led the choir and the mandolin orchestra.

I would like to say several words about organized sports among us, in town. Soccer was played on the "wygon" – a green meadow, from which one would drive away the cows that were grazing there, beforehand. During one such match, Danye Berkovitch was wounded in one of his eyes. I placed cold water on the wound and he then told me that he loved me...

Swimming and kayaking contests took place on our river, the Yaselda.

For their achievements in sports, the Jewish youth would receive prizes. The distribution ceremony would take place on the third of May, in the marketplace, against Berman's wall, in the presence of a huge crowd. The firefighters' wind orchestra played. Incidentally, the same orchestra would play at the evening dances, which would take place in the firefighters' hall. I would peek in through a crack, and used to be envious of the Kasierski sisters, the prettiest girls in town, who gracefully danced with young men to the sounds of Tango Notturno...

I learned how to dance a tango at the Resniks' home, to the music of a gramophone and a great trumpet...

And so, I finally finished school. The commencement evening of our graduation took place. We listened to several speeches. We sang, we danced, and we feasted upon the tasty food which the parents had prepared.

The mood was joyful. I received my first kiss from a boy.

We danced until late at night. We danced and we sang: "Spin, you, little wheel, spin, you, milk jug [?],[25] working diligently is no game"...

---

[25] I was unable to determine the exact meaning of the word used in the original text here: *milchele*, although *milch* means "milk," and

Working diligently... The twelve-year-old children already had to consider work regarding their future. Not everybody had the opportunity to leave for the larger cities to go study in gymnasiums[26] and in technical institutions. That cost a lot of money, and few Jews were in the position of taking such a fee upon themselves.

After completing school, I shifted about without an aim. As a tailor, I, with my two clumsy hands, was not suited; in our little shop, they could make do without me. I earned a few groschen providing co-repetitions for little children. And unfortunately, I had endless free time. I went around doing nothing.

I recall how they gave me a nickname, "Madame Simpson," on account of the fact that Nyome Broyde renounced his friends so as to be closer to me, in contrast – heaven forbid – to the British king who had renounced the crown, because of Madame Simpson. This particular sensation happened at that time.[27]

Indeed, I spent my free time well. But what next? Purpose? Here in town, there did not appear to be any solution or way out.

---

milchele is a diminutive of that word. This leads me to believe that the original term may mean "milk jug" or something related to that.

[26] A gymnasium in this context does not refer to a place for gymnastics. Throughout much of the European educational system, a gymnasium is a secondary school that prepares students for the university, much in the way that the United States offers the educational option of college preparatory high schools.

[27] This is a reference to the scandalous affair and ultimate marriage of Edward, Prince of Wales, and the American socialite, Wallis Simpson, which took place in 1937. Prince Edward abdicated the British throne in 1936 in order to marry Simpson. For further biographical details, see for instance: https://www.biography.com/celebrities/wallis-simpson (accessed 6-11-24).

Suddenly, a solution sprung out at me. An honest twist of fate in my life. Tsysho, the Central School Organization in Warsaw,[28] was offering a stipend to study (without money, it is understood) in the Yiddish gymnasium in Vilna, or in Bialystok [Białystok]. Given that I was a particularly good student, and my father was a member of the parents' committee and had yielded big earnings for the school and for social life in town, in general, they granted me the stipend.

At home we weighed Vilna against Bialystok, and arrived at the decision – Bialystok, because we had wealthy relatives there, the Babitsh family.

When my girlfriend Machlye found out that I would be going to study in Bialystok, she also decided to go study there, because she had a sister who lived there.

We were ready to skip a grade of gymnasium; and furthermore, during the summer, we took courses in German and Latin with a Polish student who was spending her summer vacation in Bereza.

However, a misfortune happened here. Machlye's twenty-year-old brother, Hershel, suddenly died, and we interrupted our studies for a period of time. The town's entire Jewish youth attended the funeral of the handsome, talented young man.

I diligently prepared myself for my arrival at the Bialystok Yiddish gymnasium and could not wait for the day when that would happen.

---

[28] For additional information about this Jewish school organization, established in Warsaw in 1921, see: https://yivoencyclopedia.org/article.aspx/Tsysho (accessed 6-11-24).

Machlye also prepared herself to go study in Bialystok, following the days of mourning for her brother.

In Bialystok

Even before the beginning of the school year, I went with my father to visit Bialystok to get a look around. My father needed to purchase merchandise for the shop and took me along. For a student, one did not need to purchase a train ticket. And so why should I not take advantage of such an opportunity to become acquainted with the city and the conditions under which I would need to study and take the first independent steps of my life?

I got to know my relatives. My aunt was in an exalted mood – she had decided to visit her children in Paris. We accompanied her to the train. When she was already standing on the small landing of the wagon, my father said that I would be coming to Bialystok and that I would be living with them. She did not hear this; she closed herself off – tuning this out – and did not react. My father visibly weighed not telling her everything; that he had chosen to "abandon" me at their home...

It was the evening prior to the beginning of the school year. I was ready for the trip. I was dressed. The suitcase goods with the most necessary items and a bundle of bedding – I placed in the carriage, where Machlye was already sitting with her packed belongings. We drove to the Bereza train-station in Bludnye. I said goodbye to my father and mother and my little brothers. My mother cried. Of course, it hurt her heart to send away her young daughter, alone and by herself, to a large, foreign city. In addition to her worry and also to all of our disappointment, a delayed telegram from my aunt arrived there immediately prior to my departure, saying that I should not come to them and that I should wait for a letter.

I grew afraid that nothing would come of my further studies, and with tears in my eyes I asked that they still allow me to go. Until today, I do not understand my father, why he did not accompany me, so as to get me settled in a foreign place. However, I had decided to begin the struggle with life's hardships. This contest was addictive; it ignited my fantasy and my desire to overcome temptations.

And hardships, temptations let themselves be felt right away. It was not an easy step for two young girls to go out for the first time into the wider world. The trip to Bialystok took a long time. We needed to transfer in Brisk and schlep ourselves with our packed belongings to another train. Finally, we arrived. Machlye's sister, Leah, and her husband, greeted us amicably in Bialystok; giving us their own bed in a small room of their compact apartment, which consisted of this small room and a small kitchen.

We got up the following morning. It was a warm, summer morning. I took my packed belongings and went by foot to my relatives, the Babitshes. In one hand I held my suitcase (it was not heavy, because I did not have a lot of things), and with the other hand, together with Machlye, we carried the bundle of bedding. In the middle of the street, the bundle spilled out. We barely managed to pack it up and continued onward.

Amazed, small-town girls that we were, we took in the large, walled houses, the broad, noisy streets, and sidewalks. We passed Kosciuszko Place with the clock on the old, historic city hall building. We observed the Church of the Holy Spirit, which was on a hill.

The Yiddish language was heard in every corner. On the signs of the Jewish shops – Jewish names. Our hearts grew strangely warm – we were not in a foreign place... Our saliva was running as we stood next to the display window of a chocolate and confectionery shop, or a bakery, seeing the decorated tortes with cream and chocolate, which had been put on display...

Finally, we finished the long trek from Sienkiewicz Street to Kolejowa, to the Babitshes. They ran a large grocery store and had a yard with several double-storied residences. The daughters and their families ate lunch with their parents. A maid oversaw the housekeeping. They took me in coldly and immediately placed me in the kitchen to wash dishes. They wanted to make a delivery girl of me in their store. About me they claimed that when one has no money, one has no business studying further. The Bereza school was already enough. And right away they spirited me away to their in-laws, the Levins, who were then at their country house, and there was a place there to sleep.

It was the first time in my life that I remained alone by myself. I looked over the apartment. And here – a terrifying experience. In one of the rooms, I found a dead person. It was a sub-tenant whose wife had left him to God's salvation... As an addition, there was a cat that pestered me, meowed, and made my bedding wet. From all these things I was shaken up from terror and cold on the hard couch in the large salon, where I was going to stay overnight. Not having any choice, I remained there.

The following morning, I went with Machlye on foot to our gymnasium on Fabryczna Street. In the large yard – the building of the gymnasium, and also, a small textile factory. And there was a racket from the students who were standing there along with the vehicles, which could be heard through the open windows of the small factory.

The secretariat of the gymnasium took care of the formalities and sent us self-examinations in German and Latin. We survived the difficulties of both examinations, were accepted by the gymnasium, and thus found ourselves in class a day later. All the faces were new to us. The students looked at us with curiosity, getting to know us. They introduced themselves: Ite Shulman, Nyunye Brodsky, Aron Tishler, Chaimke Gilinsky, Moyshe Yovarkovsky, and many others. Machlye and I sat together on a single bench.

At gymnasium, matters were regulated. We continued with our studies, which interested me from the first day onward. But my living conditions... The landlord of the apartment where I slept, Levin, was an older Jew with a little white beard. His wife was a thin, bent-over woman. She right away asked me to clean, wash, and scrub the apartment, which stood empty, while they were away at their country home. They put aside a little bed in the kitchen for me to sleep on. Insofar as providing food, there was nothing to speak of. They did not even invite me to have a glass of tea. For the hard work that I performed for my "inviting guests," I did not receive a single broken groschen, not a thank you, nor even a friendly smile. My tears would run into the dirty bucket of water, as I washed the floors, and during the nights, they would wet my pillows. Apparently, it was my relatives' decision to take advantage of me as a maid, as a charity for allowing me to sleep on the hard little bed in the kitchen.

I did not write my parents about all of this. I was afraid that they would call me back home. I preferred to go about hungry, rather than go eat at the Babitshes, where they viewed me as a nuisance or an affliction.

With impatience, I would await the mail, the Sabbath package from home, which my brother, Berele, would prepare for me and take by sled to the post office. It was already winter. In the package I would always find a piece of chicken, a piece of gefilte fish, white cheese, a pickle, a jar of preserves, a piece of cake, and a piece of chocolate with a zloty, wrapped in a small piece of paper. For that zloty, one could purchase five black rolls, instead of four white ones. It was seldom that I permitted myself to buy sausage for five groschen in the elegant café, which almost for the sake of angering me, was located just next door.

On a Wednesday one could consume a lunch at the home of one of my teachers: lentil soup with a matzoh ball and a cutlet. I recall that from Passover until summer vacation, I allowed myself such a luxury three times. In gymnasium, saliva would run from my mouth, as I watched students purchasing cheese or poppyseed cookies during the long recess. Up until today, whenever I see such baked goods, I buy them right away...

My girlfriend, Ite Shulman, definitely noticed that I was almost always hungry. And so, she would treat me with a roll and sprats. Her parents, both doctors, ran their own clinic and were well-off. Apparently, bearing the feeling of all that was happening across Europe, but especially, so that their son would be able to study in a school of higher education, they left for America just before the Second World War.

The hungry days and the difficult work that I had to do in order to be allowed to remain where I was staying were compensated for by the pleasant hours spent in gymnasium. Interesting studies, and good, sincere teachers. Hirshfeld, the director of the gymnasium, once pulled my hair and warned me that students may only stroll about on the streets until ten o'clock in the evening, and that he saw me with a youth at eleven o'clock at night. Yes, there was such an occasion. The fellow tried to draw me into a left-wing youth organization, wanted to persuade me that one must overthrow the ruling power and put an end to the exploitation of the workers, lead such an order as in Russia, which would allow all people to prosper, among them, also the Jews...

During an examination, the director whispered to me that one's lot, fate, is the leading force in Greek mythology. Taking that thought with me, I thought to myself that until now fate had served me well. I became a student of the gymnasium, and skipped a class, after passing the examination for Latin and German, as Machlye and I had had in mind.

We learned everything in Yiddish, and this made things much easier. Hebrew, we did not learn in great depth. Compared to the

Bialystok city students, I knew the Polish language poorly. In Bereza, Yiddish was spoken everywhere, so I had problems translating words from Yiddish into Polish.

In general, discipline prevailed over the classes. There was an exception regarding our relationship to the Latin teacher. She was strict, angry. And so, the jokesters responded to her intrinsically: they gave her a nickname – "The Mufti," and how many times there were that they wrote on the chalkboard prior to her arrival in class: "The Mufti is coming!" I had bad feelings about her. I would not do the homework. One time, the best student in class, Yovarkovsky, wrote the homework assignment in my notebook. The teacher caught it right away and justifiably made a big ruckus.

My difficult living conditions came into conflict with my studies. I would mostly do the homework during recess, or I would write it [up] on my knee during a boring lecture, because at home I was always very tired following the difficult day in class and the slavery of the Levins.

During recess we would often sing: Manger's "Rabbeinu Tam,"[29] Polish "hits": "The Last Sunday," "You Are a Little Table for Me," and others. Youth remains youth and wants to sweeten every free minute. I had to, as previously mentioned, take care of the homework during recess.

The German teacher, Gelroth, was very pleasant toward me; an honest, attentive, good friend. She was dedicated to teaching, and taught with fervor; and also, with much success. Her relationship toward her pedagogical obligations did not change

---

[29] This is a reference to the writer and balladist, Itsik Manger (1901-1969), and the text he composed for this Yiddish song. For further information about the song and its lyrics, see: https://yiddishsongs.org/rabeynu-tam/ (accessed 6-11-24).

our "rebellion" against her sharp rigor and our singing her an especially thought-up satirical "[La] Marsigliese" with our class. The jokesters would also play pranks. Once, during class, she placed the class notebooks on the hot oven, and searched for them, searched for them... Insofar as I was concerned, she wondered why I neglected my studies. She told me this when we met each other on the way to school. I told her how difficult it was for me; and not being able to contain myself, I cried bitterly. It was the first time that I complained to somebody.

The teacher took control of my situation. She created three co-repetition hours for me. The students lived in various corners of the city, and I would go on foot to them in the most major snow and rain, so as to save the few groschen of transportation expenses.

Up until today, I recall the friendly family on Bialostoczek Street, where they would treat me during the class to a glass of hot tea and preserves, which warmed my limbs and stilled the hunger from which I always suffered, a bit. They had one daughter, a girl who limped; and were happy that I patiently tutored their child.

On my way to a student on Swietego Rocha Street, I would sometimes allow myself the luxury of buying the tasty Bialystok cake squares and eating them right away on the street.

The money that I earned from these hours of work allowed me the possibility of ridding myself of the Levins.

In the house where Machlye lived, I, together with Michlye Kaplan – also a girl from Bereza – rented a cheap little room beneath a crooked roof. We, the three girlfriends, often got together, went to the movie theater, which was in the same yard, and saw good films.

I would save several groschen from my food and buy a ticket to a Yiddish theater performance. That was for me a real holiday [i.e., treat].

Jewish social [political] party and cultural life bustled in Bialystok. The best theater ensembles played guest roles. Well-known Yiddish writers, cultural activists, singers, and musicians appeared. The war between the parties was big on the Jewish street. Especially prior to the elections for city hall. I recall how I distributed election slips for the Bund and pushed one into the hand of our gymnasium director, who was a well-known Left Poalei Zionist.

Once in the evening, I was at my girlfriend's house. Suddenly, a Polish detective appeared who searched all of us. It turned out that the apartment belonged to a well-known Communist family...

I did not return home during winter vacation. I did not have any money for a train ticket. My earned money was only sufficient to pay for a room. Only for Passover did Michlye and I finally return home. A truck took us free of charge. We traveled by night through the Bialowieza Forest. A terrifying darkness. In addition, a frightening secret pressed down upon me: Michlye's mother had committed suicide, and Michlye would likely not return to Bialystok... Her mother was tubercular and had been convalescing in the Otwock Forests. When she returned home from the convalescence home, she realized that her husband, the baker with one foot, had betrayed her with Freidele, their maid, who indeed, later had a child by him. After his wife hanged herself, the baker married Freidel.

Both of my girlfriends, Machlye and Michlye, were later imprisoned together with their families, confined in the Bereza Ghetto, and murdered along with all the local Jews.

On account of my returning home for Passover, the gymnasium took away the leading role from me in the performance, "The Second Gate," a children's play by Halina Gorska. However, I recited a part of Peretz's, "A Night at the Old Marketplace," and participated in other scenes.

I took part in assembling the study, "A Hundred Years of Polish Jewry," within the context of our schoolwork.

With the gymnasium we went on an excursion to Gdynia and Gdansk. According to a decision made by the general school meeting, the students from Bereza were released from paying travel expenses. We saw the sea [i.e., Baltic], the port, and new big cities. Traveling by ourselves by train was an experience for us small-town young adults. For me, it was like a world had opened up, about which I only had a particular notion from books that I had read. And here – I saw so much with my own eyes!

In the meantime, I had a piece of good fortune. It was thanks to the student Naomi Glogowski, who took me into the Reisner family. He [Mr. Reisner] was an editorial assistant at the Bialystok Yiddish newspaper. Mrs. Reisner was especially sweet toward me; she would make sure that I washed myself with hot water and gave me tasty meals. The uprising of the Bialystok Ghetto was later organized at their place, at Chmielna 2. Their daughter, Nechama, my girlfriend, and their little boy, were murdered during the Nazi murders. Reisner survived.

The Germans dragged him off to do labor in their secret print shop for counterfeit banknotes. I later read his book regarding the destruction of the Bialystok Ghetto.[30]

---

[30] The book referenced here that was authored by [Refael] Rayzner [Reisner] is *Der umkum fun Byalistoker Yidntum, 1939-1945* [The

I do not recall how exactly I came to know Itzel Stam, a student from Gutman's gymnasium. In the evenings we would take strolls while holding hands. I, and my one and only festive dress, which had been remade from a dark blue silk coat. I would always pin on a small rose or some other flower with a pin, rather than with jewelry. He – in his gray-blue gymnasium uniform – a black-haired, well-built, pleasant-natured young man. In a dark corner beneath a tree, I received my first kiss from him. That evening, it took me a long time to fall asleep. I lay in bed intoxicated, with open eyes, swept up in a sweet haze. Thanks to him, on our walks, I got to know Bialystok, which bustled with Jewish cultural life. We wandered about across the poor, urban Jewish quarters – the sand, the evergreens. From every one of my meetings with him, I returned home in a good disposition, happy, and waited impatiently for the next get-togethers.

And now, we had already reached the end of the school year. Itzel completed gymnasium and received his Matura,[31] and I intended to return home. The crowd got together at my home. Itzel rented a carriage, which through outside roads brought us to the train depot. On the way, we sang, happily making a din. Itzel distributed tickets to everyone on the train platform, and the crowd accompanied me into the wagon.

Itzel intended to immigrate with his own family to South America. I do not know if they succeeded. I never again saw any more of my dear school chums. I said my farewells to them for

---

Destruction of the Bialystok Ghetto, 1939-1945]. It was published by the Bialystoker Centre in Melbourne, Australia, in 1948.

[31] The Matura is the final or exit examination administered to high school students in Poland. One must pass this exam in order to continue one's studies at the university or at some other institution of higher learning.

good at the Bialystok train station in the summer of 1939, on the eve of the frightening Second World War.

I now know that my girlfriend from class, Ite Shulman, is in America and Naomi Glogowski is in Australia. Leike Jedwab is in Paris. The names of several of my friends from the Yiddish gymnasium are mentioned by Berl Mark in his book about the uprising of the Bialystok Ghetto.[32]

---

[32] This is a reference to the following book, which was written in multiple languages: Bernard Mark, *Der oyfshtand in Bialistoker geto: loyt der tsveyter oyflage fun Yidishn historishn institut in Poyln: mit a spetsyeln nokhvort fun mekhaber* (Buenos Aires: Ikuf, 1953).

The Second World War Breaks Out

I arrived in Kartuz-Bereza before day. I crawled tiredly into my mother's bed. I rested up very well and already, I was running out into the street to meet with my gang, which had returned home from Vilna, Pinsk, and Bialystok: Vovik and Mulik Levinson, both Nyome Zackheims, Lozer Shtuker, Sarale and Moyshel[e] Resnik, Itzel Goberman, and others.

We spent the summer well – at the river, in the forest, strolling along the avenue. My parents were proud; when the neighbors proposed that I spend an hour a day with their children, and it is understood, they immediately agreed to this. I, conversely, was not enthusiastic about this – once again working, instead of spending my time carefree. Didn't they understand, my parents, that I was deserving of a little rest and enjoyment following such a difficult year of study and living in want?

Eight children got together to learn. The final hour was spent at the photographer's, Eshman. As usual, there was a din there from the peasants, who would come there to make passport photographs just prior to their departure for South America – Uruguay, Brazil, Paraguay – with the hope of finding a livelihood and improving their thread of life. When it was quiet in the waiting room, I would take a nap in the mid-hour, out of tiredness, in the great leather sofa.

It was best at the home of our neighbor, Dr. Arian, a good, nice-looking, interesting person. His wife, much older than he was, supported him while he studied medicine. As a doctor, he was successful, and had a large practice. The prettiest women in the neighborhood liked going to him to be cured. Loose tongues would wag that his pretty maid had to keep her bed clean, because he was a frequent guest by her... I had to spend many hours with his eight-year-old son, Witek. So, I would read books with him, dictated to him, or simply schmoozed with him at the round table in their beautiful garden.

The cherry tree in the doctor's garden, with its juicy fruit, would not let me be. So indeed, one time, I climbed up on the tree and put the cherries straight into my mouth. The window to Dr. Arian's office was on a diagonal. So, he noticed my activities, came out, yanked me off the tree and gave me a spanking on my underside – me, the teacher...

I would pick the large, juicy strawberries in his garden while pausing on the ground, so that the doctor should not see me and catch me in the act of committing a crime...

For the money that I earned for these hours that I gave up, my parents bought me a little Moser watch with a pretty strap. That watch served me for many years. From the earned money I also paid the dentist for repairing my teeth, from which I have had problems my entire life.

And then vacation ended. I was happy that they postponed the beginning of the school year for several days. Soon, however, we understood the reason why – it smelled of war. And that is also how it was. The first of September 1939, Nazi Germany plundered Poland. The Second World War broke out.

We listened with tension as the radio conveyed the proceedings of the war, the bombings of Warsaw. Jews were terrified. Many recalled the First World War, mentioning it with a shiver. Others attempted to comfort themselves that the Germans were then good to the Jews...

In order to avoid the effects of war, a group of Jews, including my parents, decided to leave town as quickly as possible and go to the village of Sporevo, where Leizer Abramowicz and the Ratners and their families lived. This village was known, thanks to the export outside of the country of crabs, which were caught in the local lake. Following our arrival, whole buckets of potatoes were cooked for the crowd to eat, along with sour cucumbers.

Two weeks later, word arrived that the Russians, and not the Germans, were taking over our area. We returned home in pairs with much happiness, loaded up with our few belongings. On the way, we encountered peasants who beat us with sticks and threatened us with knives. We fled, and they grabbed our things, shouting: "What is yours is mine! Now there is Communism, and everything is everyone's!"

A small portion of our things, the police later searched for and returned to us.

The population, especially the Jews, greeted the Soviet military with flowers. The Soviets "extended a brotherly hand to us" and proceeded on to White Russia. Life in our town had now changed entirely. The shops were closed. Our little shop was also liquidated. The marketplace grew empty – no more fairs, no more market days, no more business transactions. My father, fortunately, obtained a government position. My mother became a cashier in a cookshop, which opened within a wall of the marketplace.

The Soviet powers forced the well-off inhabitants to give away a portion of their residences and be satisfied living with crowdedness and common labor. The concentration camp was again transformed into barracks for army units, now – Soviet ones.

The first one to open the camp gate in the beginning of September 1939 was Michał [Michael] Semyon. The Poles had him confined here for Communism, several weeks prior. The watchmen of the camp disappeared, so the arrestees thrust open the gate and fled in every direction, not allowing themselves to remain in Bereza for even one moment longer.

The peasants from the surrounding villages plundered the concentration camp and robbed the granaries, which were full of food. The Jews from Bereza assembled themselves, creating some sort of order in town. One of them, Kamenetzky, was killed in the chaos.

And at this point I would like to convey Michał [Michael] Semyon's tale about the Bereza concentration camp during the final weeks of its existence.

In August 1939, once it had become evident that Hitler was planning to conquer Poland, many youths who were disposed to the revolution demanded weapons, so as to stage an uprising against the Germans. The Polish forces ordered all the youths to be arrested and interned in camps.

The police in Bialystok and the surrounding area arrested hundreds of such youths and confined them in the city prison. Afterward, they were loaded onto cattle wagons without food and drink and not permitted to speak amongst themselves. The train did not delay the entire night and arrived at dawn in Bludnye, the Bereza train station. Here, the wagons were opened, and the people were ordered to stand four in a row. Surrounded by military, they were driven from the depot to the Bereza-Kartuz concentration camp.

Everyone remained standing at the gate, which was hemmed in by barbed wire. A policeman came out of the camp and warned that in the camp one was strongly forbidden from speaking; there were no requests, nor any complaining. Every order had to be followed without any opposition – promptly and on the spot.

Semyon related how, placed in two rows, they fled through the gate and into a long type of corridor of barbed wire. At the sides stood police, and they beat the heads of the people who had been brought in. Woe is to that, that they fell so quickly. They simply threw the dead person in "Death Place No. 1."

Under a roof, in the camp buildings, these people would be driven in only at night. Standing there with swollen feet, they needed to survive the night. In the morning – "exercises" on the spot. Furthermore, without a stop, they received blows from the policemen and their accomplices – the criminal arrestees.

One time during the day they distributed food – up to one hundred grams of glutinous bread and a half a liter of cooked bran. The "exercises" consisted of digging up ditches, placing the people therein and covering them up to the throat, so that only their head should stick out. Afterward, digging up the soil, taking the person out of the ditch, and placing another one in its place. Whenever a policeman noticed somebody fainting or suffocating, unable to breathe, he would demand that the person be removed, but that another one should be placed immediately in his place.

Behind every building there was a very deep ditch, over which lay a thick board. This was the toilet. So as to empty their human needs, they would bring over a line of arrestees. Upon command, they were forced to go up onto the board. A policeman would count until three, and everyone had to finish going down, or else – they would get a stick over their head, which a criminal hooligan was appointed to wield against them.

They would not allow the arrestees to wash the wounds on their heads, and there is nothing to speak of letting them heal. People here changed so much that acquaintances did not recognize one another. Curious how a German airplane would often throw down proclamations, stating that through them, they would soon be liberated...

Nineteen days and nights the Polish policemen so tortured the people in the Kartuz-Bereza concentration camp. During the night of the 18th of September 1939, one could hear in the cells that doors were opening up and that people were being taken out through them. Thereafter, one heard a shot. Seventeen arrestees were shot. The police did not demonstrate anything further. They received an order to flee because the powers that be were changing.

The Germans or the Russians had to arrive. At four o'clock in the morning all the doors were still locked and sealed. However, one no longer saw the police at the watchtowers.

In the camp, one heard running, a knocking at the white eaves, and the shouts: "You are free! The hooligans ran away!" This is what the internees who were full of initiative declared to their brothers-in-suffering, that the salvation had come.

The arrestees shot outside, went over to the gate, so as to tear themselves out from the surrounding wire. However, Ukrainian nationalists – followers of Bandera[33] stood against the gate and blocked the way, claiming that just as soon as the Germans arrived, they would select whom to allow out and whom not.

In front of the camp, however, peasants also gathered together from the surroundings, along with Bereza residents with some weapons, and drove out the Ukrainian hooligans.

The internees grabbed one of the chief police accomplices, the criminal outlaw who would beat the arrestees to the point of death – particularly, next to the toilet, counting to three, that the

---

[33] "Bandera" refers to Stepan Andriyovych Bandera (1909-1959), a revolutionary politician and one of the leaders of the Ukrainian national movement in Western Ukraine (Galicia), who headed the OUN, or Organization of Ukrainian Nationalists.

people should finish up. Now, they counted to three, and threw the outlaw into a ditch that was used as a toilet.

At the gate stood Polish, Jewish, and White Russian women and men with full baskets, who threw themselves upon the throats of freed relatives and acquaintances; they kissed one another and cried... Among the first ones to tear themselves free was, as previously mentioned, Michał [Michael] Semyon, from whom we learned of the above frightening details.

Under Soviet Conditions

Nazi Germany occupied Poland. Sorrowful regards came to us concerning the fate of the Jews. On the western front it was calm. With the Soviet Union the Germans had a non-attack [i.e., non-aggression] pact. In Bereza [Kartuska], which is, in general, situated in the other portion of Poland that was taken over by the Soviets, life functioned under new conditions. Red flags, placards, propaganda. People spoke of freedom and arrests were made of "enemy [or hostile] elements" – well-off residents, leaders of "reactionary" political parties... It grew increasingly difficult with food products. Nearly all the merchandise had vanished from the stores. But Jews were happy, at least not the Germans. People lived with the present day. We, the youth, certainly did not think about tomorrow. We sang the new Soviet songs, full of encouragement and joy...

At our home, new furniture that my parents bought from the Poles – "Osadniki"[34] – appeared, which the Russians drove out for being untrustworthy elements. They brought a plush, small sofa, a dresser, and a small table with a radio into my room. There were buffets in the dining room and in the kitchen. A rug from Zakopane was hung on a wall in the bedroom of my father and mother.

My parents were scarcely at home. So, my friends enjoyed getting together in my room. One time, I counted eighteen boys and five girls. We would talk about our studies in the larger cities, relating how we would spend our free time there; and it goes without saying, we would heartily sing the Soviet songs...

The fellow I liked at the time was Lozer – an intelligent fellow who studied in Vilna, was a leader in "Hashomer Hatzair."

---

[34] These were Poles who were resettled or deported from a particular region in northern Poland, which was part of the Pomeranian Voivodeship.

Unfortunately for me, it turned out that he had a girl in Vilna, and he advised me to "rip out the tooth that hurt me" – that is to say, to forget about him. Lozer was later on in the Bereza Ghetto police. Afterward, he fled to the partisans, who meted out a death sentence upon him in the forest.

Our greatest joy then was – dancing. We would dance on a circular, wooden floor in the priest's garden, beneath the sounds of the trumpet orchestra of the Bereza firefighters.

A cultural club was established at Berman's wall. There, we published a wall newspaper and prepared performances and concerts. We would have literary artistic evenings. And everything, it goes without saying, was colored by Soviet propaganda.

We were all young and without a worry, healthy, and happy, notwithstanding that worlds had overturned. Following Poland, Hitler sharpened his nails on all of Europe, on the entire world.

And we had a good time. I was popular among the boys. Nyome Zackheim sent me his diary, in which he always had something about me to write, every day. For example, the red dress was befitting for birds...

The young Soviet officers who resided in our town would court the girls. Leikele Berkovitch married an officer, rather young; and indeed, thanks to that, saved herself. Lieutenant Derevyagin, a good-looking, young Russian, also drew close to me. When my father learned of this, he grabbed me for a walk, and I received a real dressing-down.

די אױטאָרין אין בערעזע, 1941

Photo caption reads: The authoress in Bereza, 1941

Two boys, Itzel Goberman and Moyshele Bernstein, would spy on me wherever I stood and went. Itzel gave me a photograph of himself with a paraphrase from Mickiewicz's "Pan Tadeusz": "You are health alone. Your worth can only ever be known by one, who has lost you…"

Moyshele Bernstein would speak with me about literature; saying much about Rabindranath Tagore, and would relate poetically-descriptively, that he, Moyshele, was prepared to give away a glassful of his blood to me… Even then, he already drew very beautifully, drawing placards for the Soviet holidays. One felt that a talented painter was growing here.

Everything was good and nice. However, one had to think about practical matters – studying further. And in Bereza, no high school had yet been organized. The decision was made: I would go to study in Pruzhany, a district town with several high schools – either Polish, or Hebrew, which under the Soviets became a Jewish high school. Incidentally, my uncle, the Yiddish writer, Yosl Babitsh, resided in Pruzhany.

However, I lived at the home of my girlfriend, Chayekele Glaser. Although the Glasers were not well-off, they took me in to live with them for a few months, until I was better settled, and they shared with me their bit of krupnik [mushroom barley soup] and piece of black bread. As far as I recall, my parents paid them truly little. And so up until today, I am critical of myself that I did not understand that for them, I was an eternal burden.

Chayekele's father, Yitzchak-Ezra Glaser, was later arrested by the Soviets because he was an active Bundist. Seeing as I did not learn a complete school year in the Pruzhany high school and the study program was established in accordance with the Soviet system as ten classes, instead of placing me in the ninth grade, they demoted me to the eighth grade, and I lost a school year.

I left Pruzhany in a bad mood.

When the Germans captured the town a year later, they engulfed it within the Third Reich. The Jews were not immediately murdered. Later, a year later, the Jews were deported to Auschwitz, and only a few survived. Among them – the pharmacist's daughter, Beba Epstein-Sklyar. In Auschwitz, she and the chemistry teacher, Barbel, thanks to their knowledge of chemistry, were given the task of promoting synthetic rubber plants and reaped the benefits of having a better relationship [more positive interactions] with the Germans.

Bundism, and the Bund, as it is known, was then recognized among the Soviets as "the greatest enemy of the proletarian revolution..." The entire Glaser family was then driven out on the spot to Kazakhstan and was sent to a small town. All their possessions, from which the Russians of the Soviet Union to whom their residence was handed over, benefitted, remained in their home. Today, Chayekele resides with her husband and daughters in Australia. Yisroelik Glaser – in New York. The father was certainly murdered. I always mention this dear family with a deep sense of thanks.

I spent the winter vacation in Bereza and had a good time with male and female friends. New Year approached and one had to return to Pruzhany.

I returned on a frosty night. The train, however, did not bring me to my destination but rather, dropped me off in Zhabinka. I had to wait for a train to Pruzhany nearly an entire day. So, I walked around upon the snowy streets of the town with a fresh loaf of bread in my hands, which stilled my hunger.

In this manner, I came late to the final repetitions [i.e., a type of recital, often for the memorized repetition of poetry] for the school evening [i.e., a festive event or affair held in the evening], which we had prepared, and the director shoved me out from the steps leading outside. Yet, in either case, I had become hoarse from that topsy-turvy journey to Pruzhany, so it did not bother me that much.

The dance evening for the New Year get-together was jovial, and I received, according to the number on my dress, many notes with declarations of endearment.

The following school year of 1940-1941, I went to study in Kosava, a town not far from Bereza. In Kosava we had relatives, and they, in fact, helped me get settled in.

I lived with a widow and slept on the lounge chair in the dining room. In a small room of that same apartment, Soviet officers, Russians, were quartered.

In Kosava I attended a White Russian [Belarusian] school. I had to learn White Russian, its grammar and literature. It was not difficult for me. Russian was also studied here.

In general, I enjoyed my studies. And in addition, I enjoyed my free time. I would sing, participate in the school evenings. My parents paid my landlord punctually. For the final month, however, they did not manage to pay. Before I returned home following the school year, I left behind a shrine for the landlord – my belongings.

Here, in Kosava, I completed the ninth grade of the ten-grade high school, received my certificate with "excellent" in all areas of study, took my bundle of bed linens, and after saying my farewells to male and female friends, I went home for summer vacation, not realizing that we were saying goodbye forever.

It is worth noting here a rare war episode against the Hitlerist conqueror, which was played out in Kosava. Partisans attacked the Germans who were stationed in the town, liquidating them to a certain degree, driving them out, and holding the town in their own hands, for a month's time. This occurred in August 1942.

June 1941. School vacation had begun. The beautiful summer in Bereza had awaited me with all of its pleasures: the Yaselda River, its green shores, the beautiful forests with blueberries, the orchards with the juicy papirovka apples and berries, the black cherries, and red strawberries, the fresh rolls and bagels with butter, the pitchers of buttermilk and cream, the delectable cookies and delicious ice cream – everything for which I so longed in my half-hungry existence in foreign places. I wanted to go dancing again in the evenings, see and hear good Russian artists and singers who often played guest roles; to meet with my friends and have each of us tell the other how our school year had passed.

It was *bashert* [preordained, destined] for me to enjoy the warmth of my home for only a few numbered days. Suddenly, war! Nazi Germany attacked the Soviet Union, within whose borders Bereza was included, following the downfall of Poland.

War

The 22nd of June 1941. Sunday. A beautiful summer day. School vacation. A company of youths, we decided to get together by us, everyone with their bicycles, and go to the woods to gather blueberries and have a good time. The Levinson brothers, the Zackheims, Lozer Shtuker, and others, came. Vovik brought nasturtium flowers and placed them in a vase upon the radio in my room. Somebody related that on the road, one had seen vehicles with wounded people who were being brought from Brisk.

We were in a state of much suspense. What was happening? Perhaps war?

At twelve o'clock during the day, the Soviet Minister of the Exterior, Molotov, in his radio speech, declared that Nazi Germany had fallen upon the Soviet Union and declared war...

There could be no discussion insofar as the excursion in the woods. The gang dispersed in a downtrodden mood. My friend Vovik came to me again following lunch, to schmooze with me, and get advice on what to do. I never again saw any of the others.

Suddenly, a German airplane flew through and dropped down bombs on our town. We learned that there were victims. Our family hid in the garden, beneath the trees.

Around ten o'clock at night my father decided to leave Bereza, after having seen how the Russians were leaving the town in a state of chaos, taking with whatever they could of their things.

And just as we were deciding to flee, a neighbor advised me to put on a silk summer dress, and upon that – my winter gymnasium uniform; upon that – my summer coat and my mother's winter coat. I heeded the advice. I put on my nicest shoes with the low heel – new and not comfortable. In my bosom

I placed the sack with the little jewelry that I had, my school certificate and several photographs. Our father distributed up to one hundred rubles to us, as well as a slip of paper with the address of our relatives in Leningrad. Our mother was already there for several weeks visiting her sister, whom she had not seen for over twenty years. We said goodbye to the neighbors, who did not understand why we were fleeing and leaving behind our entire belongings in an unattended state. The beds were made, the tablecloth – on the table, fresh flowers in vases, food in the kitchen pantry, in henhouses, in granaries. In the large garden – fresh vegetables and fruit. None of the neighbors wanted to take the keys to our home...

Just then, a wagon passed by with Russians. Father stopped them and threw my bundle of bedding from Kosava into the wagon, which I had still not managed to unpack. He placed Leizer therein. Berele he took on the edge of his bicycle, and I sat down on my bicycle with the broken pedal and the saddle, which turned in all directions.

A dark night. One did not see any light ... We never looked at our home again.

At ten o'clock we fled, not knowing that the German was extremely close. Later on, we learned that at five o'clock dawn, the Nazi soldiers entered the town.

We moved slowly along the periphery of the road – heading east. Beyond the town we saw Soviet tanks. In the darkness, every little while it seemed to me that I was traveling up, onto a self-loading rifle or a whole stick standing upon a stone or a sand heap. We searched for the way to the former Polish-Soviet border.

In the town of Stolpce we slept over a few hours on a hard bench, met with acquaintances and relatives, and traveled further.

By day, the road was even more full of Soviet Army people and civilian refugees who had stopped off there. I met several youths from our town. We then traveled one behind the other. It was, however, difficult to keep ourselves together. From time to time a German airplane would descend lower, literally over our heads, and shoot down upon the road. We threw away our bicycles and hid ourselves in a ditch, or along the edge of a forest, alongside the road. Following one such shooting, I remained all alone, huddled within my winter coat. My father was not there, my little brothers were not there. I saw the wagon in the middle of the road. And inside of it lay a shot, unfamiliar woman, and her husband extracted from her bosom a bundle of money. I also saw from the distance, how a parachutist was descending; it turned out, a German. I became frightened, and on my broken bicycle, somehow, rode on, onward… Upon a little river lay a narrow board. I drove over it like an acrobat in a circus. In a forest I once again slept for several hours, huddling in my coat, although outside it was summer. I woke up and did not have anything to eat and drink. I went along the road. I begged at peasant huts for a piece of bread, a drink of water, and did not always receive this. Russian soldiers treated me with hard bread biscuits. One soldier gave me a few rubles.

On the way, I met a familiar Russian soldier from Kosava. We stopped and schmoozed. A higher officer with a revolver in his hand stopped both of us. He suspected that I was a spy. But when he heard from the soldier and also from his other comrades the same version about me and our acquaintance from Kosava, he told me in a friendly manner to ride on.

On the way, I encountered a young man from Bereza. And so, we then rode together. We arrived at the former Soviet-Polish border. An officer detained the refugee masses and would not allow anyone into the Soviet Union. I begged him that he allow me and my "little brother" to keep going. Following a heated consultation, word came from the officer to allow the girl through.

They also allowed the young man through. We rode hastily across the wooden border bridge and saw how a German airplane bombed the area. With all our efforts, panting and frightened, we rode on. We rode through bombed-out settlements, burning huts. We schlepped ourselves, exhausted, without energy, and arrived in Bobruisk. The local Jews sweetly took us in and gave us something to eat. They allowed us to bathe, to stay overnight.

In the morning, one could hear how the German bomber airplanes were drawing closer. So, we moved further on our way.

A truck was ready to take us, but without the bicycles. The young man from Bereza did not want to part with his bicycle. However, me they took with my bicycle. I rode with them until the intersection of Homel [or Gomel] and Mogilev. There, I went into a restaurant to catch my breath. A Jewish woman pushed small, fresh cakes into the pockets of my coat. The coat got dirty. I, however, had something to eat.

My goal was Leningrad, to our relatives, and to my mother, who was there. I had the address on a slip of paper, which I had hidden in my bosom with my several documents. I asked myself how I was going to get to Leningrad. They demanded that I go through Orsha.

None of the refugees went in that direction. When I schlepped myself there, the city was standing in flames. I rode through empty streets, past burning houses. A dense, suffocating smoke covered the world. I wanted to flee from this hell as quickly as possible.

A bizarre picture stands before my eyes: a girl all alone, upon the unfamiliar roads of a foreign land. The terror from not knowing and of death was so great, that I did not feel hunger, nor thirst. My lips were dried up and cracked. A soldier gave me some sort of balm to smear on my lips. My feet were swollen, in wounds.

Nobody did anything to me, as they do to a girl [i.e., nobody physically/sexually assaulted me], but several times they led me to the military, where they ordered me to get undressed. What were they searching for – a spy, or simply to "play around" with a girl?

I was fortunate and encountered a truck along the road with refugees from Bereza – Russians from the Soviet military store, and with them, also a young man from Bereza, Glotserman, from the mill. They helped me climb up onto the vehicle, and all of us rode to Smolensk. One of the Russians had his little house there. At his place I rested up a bit, rested my wounded feet, stretching myself across the broad Russian oven.

We only remained there a few days because the Germans had begun bombing the city. We stayed in a place between the aerodrome, gas reservoirs, and a munitions factory. A German landing troop landed there and activated rockets to their airplanes, demonstrating the bombardment targets. It was clear that we had to flee further.

Ultimately, I threw away my broken bicycle in the middle of the street and departed on foot, in the direction toward the train depot, in a group of three: the Russians, the young man from Bereza, and me. We climbed into a freight wagon and later – into a train that was going to Moscow. At night somebody woke me up and advised me to hide my hand with the wristwatch...

I never again saw the young man from Bereza.

My goal was Leningrad. So, I switched trains and entered a wagon with mobilized men who were riding in the direction toward Leningrad. The Russians – also. I lay down, tired, and fell asleep. When I awoke, I found a gas mask and a tablet of chocolate beside me, several rubles, and a photo of the Russian. At night, he got off at a small station...

In Leningrad and Across Russia

Slowly the train drew closer to Leningrad station. I was tense, anxious; I was afraid that they would once again arrest me, as in Smolensk, saying that I was a spy: I was indeed dressed and wearing my hair differently than the girls here. I cut open my new navy blue "crocodile" shoes, on account of my swollen feet. One heel had fallen off, so I broke off the other one in order to be able to walk.

How did I look? Suspicious?

Thank God, I passed through the station in peace. I turned around, lost in the streets, and searched for my aunt, according to the address that I had safeguarded the entire time, like a regular treasure.

Suddenly, an older, good-looking woman approached me. She looked me over and asked me a strange question in Russian: Was my name perhaps Fania? I responded that in Russian, people indeed called me Fania, but in Yiddish – Faigel.

And this is where an unbelievable thing occurred: the woman grew pale and said that it was possible that she was my aunt, Chaya, or as she was now called – Clara, my mother's sister.

The surprise was great. What a coincidence! My aunt had, in fact, never seen me before. How did she come to suspect precisely me, so as to stop me and ask?

Yes, it was my aunt whom I was seeking… Were a writer to describe such an episode in his book, one would of course say: it is idle chit-chat, a fantasy. In real life, such things do not happen…

As previously related, my aunt and her husband, Dovid Goldberg, for political reasons, fled from Poland to the Soviet Union and settled in Leningrad. After Bereza had become Soviet, my mother went to stay with them. The two sisters had indeed not seen each other for more than twenty years! Having already spent a few weeks in Leningrad, my mother was already sitting in the train to return to Bereza. Because of the breakout of the war, the train would not go west, and my mother had to return to her sister.

And at this point, another miracle occurred. When my mother saw me, she nearly fainted. Could she ever have imagined that the war was taking place, and her daughter had set out alone to come to Leningrad?!

And what had happened to the rest of the family?

As is understood, I did not know where my father and both of my little brothers had gone to. I had indeed remained all alone on the road.

They immediately informed my grandmother and grandfather – my father's parents – and his sister, Lyube, and his brother-in-law, who also lived in Leningrad, about me. Until now, I had never before seen them. It was very pleasant for me to be with my new family, which took me in with a great deal of love.

Lyube and her husband – Professor Osher Yaffe – had two children. They took me all around Leningrad. I was charmed by the beautiful houses, streets, and parks. The Neva River and the Czar's palace made a colossal impression on me.

One could feel an uneasiness in the city. Mobilization. Movement of military units. They protected the monuments, so that they not be damaged, should there be any bombings. People joked that the only elephant in the zoological garden should, according to the theory of probability, be fine. However, he was killed by a bomb.

My relatives lived on Saltykov-Shchedrin Street, in the former house of a count, which had been divided into several apartments. One bathroom and one kitchen and a large table were shared by several families. The table was covered with gas lamps for cooking and baking for every family, separately.

In the conjoined apartment lived the well-known Russian writer, Kataev.[35] He asked me to relate how I had come to Leningrad and what had happened with me along the way.

In the meantime, a letter arrived from my father, which he had sent from somewhere to Leningrad. He was looking for my mother and also wanted to know what was happening with his family – his parents, sister, and brother. He had also not seen them in over twenty years.

Regarding himself he wrote that in the chaos, he had at best lost both children. Somewhere in a forest he found my brother, Leizerke, by a sheer miracle. A fleeing arrestee led him by the hand. One cannot imagine his joy to find his ten-year-old son, for whom he had fruitlessly searched along the way. With him, on the edge of the bicycle, on trains, and also, in wagons, he relocated to a kolkhoz[36] in Tambov Oblast (region) in Central Russia.

---

[35] Valentin Petrovich Kataev (1897-1986) was a Russian and Soviet novelist and playwright. For further biographical details about Kataev and a list of his publications, see:
https://www.goodreads.com/author/show/7328558.Valentin_Kataev (accessed 6-13-24).

[36] A kolkhoz was a collective farm of the former Soviet Union. See: https://www.merriam-webster.com/dictionary/kolkhoz (accessed 6-13-24).

Once we had my father's address, we decided with my mother to leave Leningrad and go to him. To tell the truth, I was upset to part with our relatives. But we said our goodbyes. My grandfather gave me a present of several gold coins. I never saw my grandfather and grandmother ever again. They were found having expired from hunger in their beds during the blockade surrounding Leningrad, which the Germans maintained for several years.

Everyone escorted us to the train, which was heading north. The trains at that time were not running directly to Central Russia. For several weeks we wandered about across stations, exhausted and hungry. Remaining without a groschen of money, without a roof over our head, we – together with my mother – tasted the true flavor of wartime's migration and wandering.

As a means of transportation, we had one possibility – in freight wagons. We sat on one of my mother's suitcases. So it was, day and night. When the train came to a halt, everyone would jump down onto the field, to relieve oneself. This took place within the full view of everyone. Nobody was embarrassed.

I very much wanted to lie down in the wagon on the plank bed overhead where the men were lying. My mother, however, would not allow me to do this. One time, I nevertheless tried, but hastily crawled down, after I felt men's hands creeping toward me.

It so happened that a young Estonian fellow moved closer to me during the night, hugged and kissed me, sought further... I was intoxicated by the sudden love playing, but right away started awake and moved away from him. He did not get angry with me. He later helped us carry the suitcase when we had to switch to another train.

We did not have anything to eat. I was not ashamed to pick up a piece of moldy bread from the dirt, or to beg for something to eat from the Russian officers. Whatever I received, I brought it to my mother in the wagon.

I could still see before my eyes the Michurinsk station. We both sat an entire night on the suitcase outside, supported by a wall, since they would not allow us into the train depot.

At six o'clock in the morning the radio began to play the Strauss Waltz, "Take a Look at What Splendor; Everything around Us Appears Quiet, Absorbed in Thought…" Peasant women appeared with baskets of juicy red raspberries, enough to make the saliva run from one's lips. The sun ascended ever higher. It grew warm, a pleasure. I stretched out my limbs and smiled to the beautiful world, how crazy everything was…

The mood grew far worse when I found the first louse on the elastic of my underwear. Alas, the lice which had befallen the wanderers [i.e., us]! I observed how a woman held her daughter's head in her lap and against a knife, knocked dead the lice she found in her hair. And was it any wonder? Masses of refugees – "straw bed-less beings" – wandered about the depot – filthy, shabby, and hungry.

Here we were at the large station Rtishchevo. There were a lot of troop transports standing here. I ran with a flask to get some cooked water – *"kipiatok"* [i.e., boiling water]. It was far to the crane. So, I crawled under the wagons so as to bypass the way. Suddenly, the train began to move, and I was under a wagon. I barely managed to jump out of there. One moment more and the train would have run me over. It is understood that I did not tell my mother about this.

Finally, we were in Tambov Oblast. My mother sent me, with my broken Russian, to find out how we could relocate to the kolkhoz, according to the address on my father's letter.

My mother was a young, healthy, and energetic woman, but everything [back] at home. She could speak Russian. But here, in the far-flung unknown, she became helpless and apathetic. I, alone, had to do everything and take care of everything.

A peasant who was carrying with him a large barrel, showed us the way to the kolkhoz, and permitted us to place our suitcase on his wagon. We followed him on foot. Along the way I begged for bread from the Russian women and also gave the wagon driver a slice. Suddenly, he began to goad on the horse, wanting to run away from us. We barely managed to grab our suitcase from the wagon. Panting, barely able to stand on our feet, we schlepped ourselves to the village upon the thick Russian black soil, which shone following the rain. Small huts were dispersed across the village. Flowers and tall sunflowers decorated the area. Wide fields of grain throughout. At the ponds somebody played an accordion. Boys and girls were frolicking about, screeching at the wagons, loaded up with cut-down grain. It was a wonderful summer day.

However, suddenly, everybody grew sad. A group of peasants accompanied a soldier to the front. The screaming and crying were like that of a funeral. People were crying for the soldier while he was yet alive.

I was enveloped by a shudder. Once the entourage had passed, we began searching for my father. In the field in which he worked at cutting the grain, somebody informed him that we were looking for him.

Great was all our joy when we saw each other. We fell down, kissing, and for a long time it was as though our tongues had been snatched away. The joy was not complete. Berele was missing. Where could he be?

Once we had recovered from the experience, my father led us to the kolkhoz.

In the village, a family of peasants gave us a room, and they managed with their other room. There was no furniture in our room, only bundles of straw upon which one sat and also slept.

The landlords would eat borscht and millet daily. We did not taste this because they simply did not invite us to partake [in their meals].

My mother and I also went to work in the field. There, we would steal peas, and at night, we would cook them in a conserves can. One time, we cooked this food during the day on Sunday, and only then did we see small white worms swimming in the soup. It did not harm us, though, and peas remained our primary food.

Along with us, in the kolkhoz, were the Bereza residents Emma and her husband, Leizer Yalom. They met my father along the way and stayed together with him. Emma would steal cucumbers, pausing on all fours in the landlady's garden. She would go to work in the field in her nightgown because her only dress, which she had on, literally split asunder. The peasants wondered because who goes into the field wearing a ball gown?...

In the kolkhoz we worked hard, from dawn until dusk. It was more difficult for my mother than for all the others. She did not have any strength for the exhausting physical toil outside, beneath the scorching sun or beating wind and rain. At the point of cutting the grain and placing it in sheaves, we realized that we had not worked as much as the norm, and so the pay was extremely low.

My father sold his good bicycle, so that there would be a little money with which to buy bread. But the main concern was regarding Berele, that we had lost him along the way. Where was he? What was his fate? Was he alive?

And see and wonder: we had waited for him! Via the Leningrad relatives, whose address my father had also placed in Berele's pocket, he learned of my father's present address. After remaining alone, fleeing from the attacking German, he schlepped himself, together with the stream of refugees, to the city of Penza. And there, he arrived at a trade school. He studied, had a roof over his head, and food.

The Germans, without a let-up, advanced. The Moscow radio speaker, Yuri Levitan, would, as often as possible, provide the names of the Soviet cities, which the Nazis had conquered. The Germans were approaching! So, we decided to move on further, eastward, deep into the Soviet Union.

My wounded feet were still swollen. One foot hurt a great deal and burned a tinder-red. So, we related this in the village; that I would need to be taken to the doctor in the city. I threw off the small amount of beans onto a wagon and went along my way. Once, I had read a small book, "Tashkent, the City of Bread,"[37] and recommended moving on in that direction.

We did not go to any doctor in the city. The compresses stilled the pain a bit and decreased the redness. And so, it remained as it was – moving! Moving on further!

---

[37] Published in 1923, this was a popular Soviet children's book by Alexander Neverov, which was translated into both Polish and Yiddish.

At the train station we saw a military troop's freight wagons, propped up with people. So, we also pushed ourselves into one of the wagons. The train left for the east. At nearly every station my father would jump down and return with full buckets of food, which he would get at the evacuation points and distribute among the refugees in the wagon. Incidentally, among them there were many Soviet Jews who had fled from their places of residence when the Germans encroached upon them.

Finally, we schlepped ourselves to Tashkent, the main city of Uzbekistan, Middle Asia. In the garden in front of the train station, wandered about thousands of people. They would not allow any refugees into the city. During the night, one could hear crying, screaming, a stampede, a struggle. Somebody was robbed and the entire crowd was disturbed by this.

We saw that lying beneath the free, truly sheer sky of Middle Asia, had no purpose. We were spent, full of despair, and the situation grew worse with every day. So, we decided: we would search further for a place of shelter. We got into a train, and after a night of riding, arrived in Samarkand, the second largest city in Uzbekistan.

In Samarkand

We found ourselves at the depot spot. Inside, they allowed only women with small children. Hundreds of refugees sat down separately on the worn-out grass of the surrounding area, and also, on the sidewalk. Most of the refugees – Jews. A small number of Russians, White Russians, and Ukrainians. They kept themselves separate. There were also some Poles there. They, however, quickly disappeared.

Not far from the depot was an evacuation point, where the refugees received a plate of soup. My father would bring a bucket of borscht from there. Berele, my brother, did not want to eat this, even being extremely hungry.

At night, the people would place their thin bundles beneath their head, because thieves would cut out a hole from a side of the bundle and pull out things. One sold an article of clothing so as to buy bread. One crawled about across the city and looked for work, even if it were difficult unskilled labor. My father found work at pumping out dirty water in a small basin. Beneath a small roof in the yard of the basin were husks heaping with rice, with which one heated up the oven. Several Jews found a place there to sleep, among them also our family. I half-lay on the brick in the small room where they would turn on the water faucet. It was difficult for me to move on account of the wounds on one of my feet. In the ambulatory area at the depot, they re-bandaged the wounds after smearing them with a salve.

I was dirty, hungry, and unkempt. In such a situation it is difficult to overcome an illness. The wounds did not heal. So, they sent me to a tuberculosis dispensary because they decided that I was suffering from tuberculosis of the bones. There, a doctor examined me. He was bewildered, hearing that we lived in an old, small, bath house. Based on the address that I gave him, he came before evening to visit me. I sat in the middle of the house and in my hand, I held a lit bamboo stick – this was our lighting.

Several Jews sat on the mountains of husks and chewed on something, one – a small potato, another – a little carrot.

The doctor did not say a word, and everyone wondered: Who is this? Only I knew that this was Doctor Aminov. He clearly came to confirm that I had told him the truth about my situation. And so, he right away told me to come to him for a visit.

When I went to him the second time, he gave me a letter for the tuberculosis sanatorium; that they should accept me into their children's division for those who are sick with tuberculosis of the bones.

My mother cried bitterly, hearing that such a terrible sickness had been diagnosed for her daughter. In reality, the doctor used the diagnosis as a means by which to put me in the hospital, so that I would benefit a little from humane living conditions. I received a roof over my head, a clean bed, a lot of food, and medical aid. He literally saved me. He also arranged jobs for my parents – in the kitchen of the same hospital. The days on which they worked they had something to eat. My mother would hide a cutlet inside of a bandage around her neck, pretending that her throat hurt her. In this manner, she would bring something for my brothers, for each of them, a piece, to eat.

Being clean and satisfied, I quickly returned to my old self, and the wounds healed. In the hospital room stood eight beds. Young girls lay in plaster casts, their feet bound to hanging bricks. Their families frequently visited them and brought with them various products [food items]. The sick children did not have any appetite, and I would get their portions of the hospital lunch – several plates of soup and many cutlets, which I would consume during the course of a day. For the sick children in my pavilion, I would sing Polish and Yiddish songs; I would recite Latin verses. And so, their parents would throw into my bed some of the food items they had brought for the sick. For the most part, I liked the large nuts that they would throw me. Yes, lying in a clean bed, being well taken care of, reading, and enjoying a good book, and taking walks in a beautiful garden – literally, a Garden of Eden!

Until the end of 1941, I was in the hospital. Thanks to my so-called serious illness, they allowed my family to remain in Samarkand. We found refuge in a garret above a barn. There were no doors and no windows there. The floor – full of holes. Our feet would fall inside of them. It grew cold, the water was in a bucket, the wet socks and the torn-up, damp shoes would freeze over. Many hours we stood outside in the line for bread with the bread cards. The gold coins and the little bit of jewelry that I had brought aided us in our time of need. We sold it, and for the money, we rented a little room – an Uzbek kibitka [mud hovel or tent] with a door and a shutter (but again, without a window), with a clay floor and a lot of spider webs on the high ceiling. No water nor sanitary facilities, it is understood, were there, and also no electricity. We also did not have any kerosene lamps.

I poured a bit of kerosene into a small bottle, stuck in a cotton wick, and placed it on the crooked, rusty barrel, which served as a table. We sat on three bricks, slept on a straw mattress on the floor, the entire family covered by a single blanket. I lay in the middle. Everyone yanked the blanket toward him or her and squeezed me so much, such that I would have to get up and sit outside in order to catch a bit of air.

Tea – cooked hot water, I would go buy at the neighborhood teahouse, where Uzbeks in their long robe kaftans would sit on the floor and drink green tea, which would be poured from a beautiful, small porcelain teapot. Instead of sugar, they would suck raisins, which they would often drop into their pockets while tasting them in the marketplace.

Small clay houses – kibitkas – there were many of them in Samarkand's Old Town. In the new part of the city there were already houses built of brick – single floor and several story walls. Abramovsky Boulevard divided the city into two parts. In the Old Town there were two old buildings – noteworthy, hundreds of years old: Tamerlan's tomb[38] and the Registan,[39] with the stunning glass adornment, mosaics in several colors. Summer in Samarkand is extremely hot. The kiosks with their Morse Beer do well. Winter – occasionally warm, occasionally, rain. Following a major rain, it would happen that the clay kibitkas would fall in. That also happened with our landlady's kibitka. Following one such rain, one wall fell in.

The Uzbeks wear warm robes in both summer and winter. Summer – to protect against the external heat, winter – to safeguard the warmth of their own bodies. The female Uzbeks would cover their faces in the "Paranja," like all Muslim women. An Ariq – a narrow water channel – cuts through and waters the area. We also had to use the water from the Ariqs for drinking. Through a rag, we would filter the green-yellow water, and afterward, we would drink it.

There were several marketplaces in Samarkand. At the large marketplace in the Old Town, the refugees, mostly Jews, would

---

[38] Gur-e-Amir, Persian for "Tomb of the King," is the mausoleum in Samarkand, Uzbekistan that houses the remains of Amir Timur, also known as Tamerlane (or Tamerlan), one of the greatest Mongol kings. For additional information about this site and accompanying photographs, see for instance: https://www.wilton-photography.com/news-stories/the-mausoleum-of-amir-timur-in-samarkand (accessed 6-13-24).

[39] The Registan is a public square in Samarkand where people gathered to hear royal proclamations. It was also the site of public executions. For images of this Unesco World Heritage Site, visit: https://whc.unesco.org/en/list/603/ (accessed 6-13-24).

walk around and sell something – a watch, a pair of trousers, shoes, and other desirables. With the money they earned, they would purchase food.

Countless fruits and vegetables were at the marketplace. Once, I bought some cherries, and a boy ran over to me and hit my hand. The cherries spilled out, and he hastily, hastily picked them up from the ground, wiped off a bit of the sand, and consumed one cherry after the next.

Many homeless children moved about in the neighborhood – hungry, forlorn, filthy. A number of them were found dead – in parks, in the kiosks. They expired from hunger and cold. The Bukharian Jews from Samarkand helped out the Jewish refugees as much as they were able. I recall the local Jewish women – their long silk dresses, with a head covering on their heads, with pretty, dark faces. It also turned out that my do-gooder, Dr. Aminov, was a Bukharian Jew. And later on, years later, I encountered him in Israel...

The residents of Samarkand did not evacuate universities, technical schools, dramatic and opera theaters, from the European sector of the Soviet Union. Also, there was a Yiddish theater here.

Jewish refugees from Poland and also from Bereza furtively approached our family. My mother would voluntarily wash lice-infested laundry. Where did we get soap? We produced it ourselves. The Bereza teacher, Yalom, who was with us, found work in a leather factory. He did not have any winter clothes. So, I gave him the winter coat that I schlepped with me from Bereza. The coat also served me here during the day to protect me from the cold. I would remain seated in the kibitka on the straw mattress shivering from cold, waiting for Yalom to return from work and give me back my coat. From his job, he would bring fat from the droppings that they would rework in the factory as leather. We would fry up the fat and pour it into a clay pitcher. After the pitcher had eroded, we decided to use up the fat in making soap.

We read in a book how to do this. Yalom bought caustic soda [i.e., lye], mixed it together with the fat, and cooked it. The compound was poured into wooden cans, where it cooled and hardened. Afterward, we would cut it into four portions, and sell the finished "soap" at the marketplace. Who? – I!

Once, a militia figure caught the big "speculator" and took her away to the nearest militia point. I, however, on the way, "lost" the pieces of "forbidden merchandise." There was no proof against me; it was impossible to charge me with anything, and they let me go free.

Berele grew ill. My mother cooked up potatoes and fed them to him. We distributed the potato water – for each one several soups within the lid of a teapot. Ten-year-old Leizerke went outside and wet his feet in cold water, so as to also get sick and get a potato... He had criticisms against the government, as to why children received so little bread for their bread cards and would ask that they precisely weigh his portion.

And again, Dr. Aminov visited us in order to assist us. He took our family along with him to his new workplace – in a kolkhoz, where he was approved to work in a hospital.

My mother was responsible here for a food store and had much grief from the rats, which would gobble up or carry off food products. There was no way to hide anything from these particular creatures. A family of mice was found in the pocket of my father's coat, which hung on the wall.

My brother, Leizerke, would often cry at night, complaining of pains. My mother, however, did not take him to any doctor from the hospital where she worked. She was bewildered, as though she had received a shock, on account of the war and our situation. Nonetheless, she did the most difficult work – harnessed a horse or an ox in a two-wheeled wagon and carried loads for the hospital. Given that I did not go to the kolkhoz and remained in Samarkand, she would sometimes bring me some butter, preserves, several potatoes, and some apricots, which one could tear off the trees, along the way.

In the meantime, my father was mobilized to the labor front, and was sent to Chelyabinsk, to the Urals.

As I said, I remained alone in Samarkand and worked for negligible pay at sorting raisins. But therefore, I was able at work to fill up on raisins.

Resumed Studies

Leizer Yalom continued to live with me. In the middle of one night, he cried out in his sleep; spoke with his young daughter who remained in Bereza, that she should not go into the fire. His heart knowingly felt from the distance that his child was in danger. He was not mistaken… He was later mobilized, and he took leave of us.

My Aunt Chaya – Clara – and her husband, Dovid, moved into my small room. They managed to flee from Leningrad and survived the terrifying blockade, which the Germans placed on the city, and also from the hunger, which annihilated hundreds of thousands of Leningrad residents. They purchased a small table and a bed for themselves. Upon the brick they placed a door, and this was my sleeping area. I had no mattress, only a clean bed sheet – yes.

When, during the rainy days [season], a wall collapsed in the landlord's hut, we took her ten-year-old son in to live with us. She herself died of spotted typhus. From her son, huge lice would crawl about on the floor. It is a wonder that we did not contract the typhus.

Aunt Clara befriended the neighbors. Among them was one Uzbek, a thief. My aunt gave him pay-off money, so that he would leave us alone.

Uncle Dovid was a shoe model. He, however, was unable to work on account of a light paralysis in his hand. From time to time, my aunt would sew up a shirt for somebody, and would receive something for this. They gradually sold off their belongings, so as to have something to eat. At the appropriate time, in Leningrad, they gave me as a gift a new pair of shoes. For a long time, I only wore one of the shoes, since the other foot was bandaged, and I wrapped the bandage with the wool pants of my bathing costume, which I put on, in order to ride on my bicycle. When my sick, left foot healed, I put on backwards – the rag, on the right foot – whose shoe had become completely stretched-out, and the whole left shoe, I placed on the healed left foot...

Opposite of where we lived, there was a school for pilots. The fellows would often schmooze with my relatives. One evening, I went for a stroll with one of them and spoke about trigonometry and other studies. In a quiet place, alongside a walled-off hedge, he suddenly threw me onto the grass. His intention was clear... So, I began to argue with him, saying that I am not nice... As an example, I withdrew from my pocket a piece of cotton. Precisely that day, I had found a piece of raw cotton wool with the seed in the middle. It interested me because until then, I had never before seen this, and I placed it in my pocket. Now, it proved useful to me. The attacker let me be.

Also, earlier on, an Uzbek tried to rape me. Occasionally, I would go by foot from Samarkand from the Kolkhoz to my family, twenty kilometers away, to see my relatives and bring some products. On the way, in the Kolkhoz, an Uzbek who worked in the field called me over in regard to taking along a letter and throwing it into a mailbox in the city. In my naiveté, I approached him. And so, he jumped on top of me, attempting to throw me down. With difficulty, I tore myself out of his filthy hands.

On the way back, my brother, Berele, accompanied me. Both of us schlepped a sack of potatoes. On the way, Berele caught a bout of malaria with a high fever. So, I needed to schlep the bag on my own and also help my brother remain upright on his feet. With our last strengths we schlepped ourselves home.

One particular day I met Nellie Polishuk – a Jewish girl from Kiev with whom I had become acquainted on the train, while en route to Samarkand. She related to me that she had been accepted as a student at an institute, and that they had summer courses there for external Matura [students].[40] Indeed, I had been unable to complete my final grade of high school.

I did not ponder, I did not consult anyone; I took a pen and in my broken Russian, wrote a request letter. I went off with Nellie to the institute, and how great was my joy when I was informed that I had been accepted to this course.

I was steeped in studying. I would sit on the three bricks, my "stool," for hours, next to the rusty barrel, my "table," and by the light of the oil lamp, I would study, and write. My body would hurt from the hard bed upon which I slept. My intestines would "play a march" from hunger... However, I bit my lips, and indeed, studied day and night.

The studying also did not come easily to me, because my Russian was poor. Nonetheless, I passed all the exams with excellent – "otlichno." Only in Russian did I receive a good – "horosho." I remember, I wrote on the subject, "Revenge within [the Writings of] Shakespeare." It was a good work, but with orthographic errors. A high school student, Petko, helped prepare me for the geometry exam, of which I was very much afraid. He was a talented fellow who left to go study ship building in the evacuated Odessa institute. He became an engineer.

Ultimately, I received my Matura [i.e., diploma]. It did not come easily to me: Bialystok, Pruzhany, Kosava, and Samarkand... Nowhere did I lick any honey. From where did I draw this strength? The endurance? The strong will? In general, I was not a young girl then.

---

[40] The Matura was (and is) the equivalent of a high school diploma in sundry European countries. However, high school was considered far more rigorous, overall, than most American high schools. Maturas were (and are) necessary for admission to university (or non-vocational schools of higher learning).

With such a good diploma, they would not allow me to leave the institute. I was advised to become a student in the Department of Technology and Economics. I agreed and began studying in a *Hochschule*.[41] Following the first semester, and having passed all seventeen of the exams, my situation radically improved. And it happened in the following manner.

Once, in the evening, the dean of the department, Professor Matinian, an Armenian, invited me into the professors' lounge. The professors were already gathered there. I sat down opposite them and covered up the large hole on my knee in my only pair of thick, black socks [or tights] with my hands. I was embarrassed and also afraid. For what reason had they called me out?

---

[41] *Hochschule* is German for an institution of higher learning. Literally, it means "high school," but in American terms, it is more closely aligned with a college or university.

פּראָפֿעסאָרן און סטודענטן פֿון סאַמאַרקאַנדער אינסטיטוט פֿאַר עקאָנאָמיע און טעכנאָלאָגיע. די אויטאָרין — דריטע פֿון לינקס אין צווייטער רײ

Professors and students from the Samarkand Institute for Economics and Technology. The authoress – third from the left in the second row

My surprise and joy were great when Professor Matinian declared for the assembled, that he had selected me as the best student, and asked everyone what their opinion was of me. Everyone agreed with his selection. So, he further declared to them that a stipend in the name of Stalin had arrived from Moscow, which only the best student could receive.

And I had received this stipend! What an honor and what good fortune! It pays to study hard. Every month I received 500 rubles, later – 700 rubles. I would hand over the money to my aunt, and we had three times enough with which to purchase bread, potatoes, and noodles. From time to time, when I did really well on an exam, I would receive potato pancakes from my aunt…

The Jewish students from Poland knew about me. In the local Polish newspaper, they drafted an article about the "Polish student" who had merited such an honor. From the Polish "Punkt"[42] I had received a present – wool for a sweater, soap, and sugar. My aunt also knitted me a sweater from an old jacket of hers. Factually speaking, I had nothing to wear. I could not even afford to purchase used goods or shoes on the open market, while the money was also supposed to support my aunt and uncle. It turned out that with my stipend, I supported three people.

With much impatience we would always await the postal carrier. My aunt and uncle both awaited letters from their two sons from the [war] front, and I – for a letter from my father from Chelyabinsk; later on, also from my brother, Berele, from the [war] front. The letter which revealed that Berele had fallen in battle beyond Warsaw, they hid from me.

---

[42] This appears to be a reference to some type of all-purpose store.

פון רעכטס: די אויטאָרין, דער ברודער בערעלע פאַרן אָפֿגיין אויפֿן פֿראָנט, די מוטער, װיכנע, דער ברודער לייזערקע

Photo caption reads: From the right: the authoress, her brother, Berele, before his dispatch to the [war] front, her mother, Vichne, her brother, Leizerke

They mobilized Berele just at the end of the war. Had he remained studying in a vocational school, or had my father taken him with him to Chelyabinsk, I believe, the war would already have ended before they would have mobilized him at the age of seventeen.

Up until today, I do not understand why my parents did not send him to go study. He had just completed the seven-grade school in Bereza and could have entered any old vocational school, and then would not at his young age have been mobilized.

He served in a regiment eight kilometers from Samarkand. I used to bring him food that our aunt had prepared. Later on, I accompanied him when his unit left for the [war] front, while singing the song, "Be well, Mother, don't be sad, wish me a good journey…" With his unit, he marched through nearly all of Poland. We received a card from him that he was going away to the first battle and that he would write. However, he never wrote again…

I will never forget my dear little brother. A good soul, a blossomed bloom that was cut down before its time. He gave up his young life to avenge the cruel murder of the large family of Polish Jews.

One time, after having returned from visiting Berele, who had been mobilized, again, eight kilometers by foot, I entered with weak steps the exam for physics and colloidal chemistry. Three girls ahead of me had flunked. I passed the exam with "very good" and continued to receive the stipend.

In order to hold on to the stipend, on more than one occasion I had to pass up on entertainment, the dances in the park, or a nice performance in the theater or at the opera. As I already said, well-known Russian theaters and operas evacuated to Samarkand. But I had one goal for myself – to study!

Vacation and Further Study

The students, during the free summertime, would walk around in the marketplace, tasting from the stalls' fruits and vegetables. With this, they would still their hunger a bit. In the kitchen of the institute, we would try in the largest bowls possible, to receive the poured-in *"zatsheruche"* [i.e., buckwheat gruel] – the thin "soup." Having poured out the water, I would eat up the thick kasha of cooked-up meal.

During summer vacation the students had to help out the kolkhozes, where there was a shortage of farm hands to harvest the grain.

Our group was brought to a far-flung hick town, quite far-removed from Samarkand. We were quartered in a forlorn structure. We spread out the wooden cot with the blankets, which we had brought with us and made ourselves a place to sleep. When I asked the girls why they did not change their undergarments for the night, they looked at me, wounded. They did not know from any nightgowns or pajamas. Given that we were not tired, we sang pretty Russian wartime songs until late in the night. I sang Polish songs, which very much pleased everyone.

A professor, a Tatar, accompanied us, so as to watch over us. At one such opportunity, he told me that he had not imagined that among Jews there were such capable types as I. That's how well he knew the Jews...

In the morning, we ran out to purchase something from the peasants. Going from cottage to cottage and purchasing sour milk and *"lepyoshkas"*[43] – a form of flour pretzel. How great was our amazement when we met a lot of people in the village

---

[43] A *lepyoshka* or *obi non* is a type of flatbread pastry common in Afghan, Tajik, and Uzbek cuisine.

without noses. It turned out that this was a place in which they had settled syphilitics, who had, as the result of this terrible sickness, for which there was at that time no cure, lost their noses...

Hearing this, we decided to get out of there as quickly as possible. When night fell, we left our blankets to the responsibility of the professor; that he bring them back to the city with a wagon, and we went on foot to Samarkand across dusty roads. A broad river blocked the way. So, we cut across the river half naked, in the dark, and reached the other bank. The moon showed itself; it lit up the area a bit, and we saw in front of us another river and that the waters from both rivers were drawing closer. And so, from there, we ran back. In the quiet of the night, we would occasionally hear the moaning of little children. Those were jackals. I heard this for the first time in my life. A shudder ran through me. All of us shivered from fear and gathered together all of our strength so as to distance ourselves from here, as quickly as possible. We searched for another path, and the entire night went astray, spent; with limp steps we finally schlepped ourselves home to Samarkand.

We were strongly rebuffed. For running away, we were not punished. Knowing that those who had sent us there understood who was correct...

Summer passed. A new year of study began. I once again studied hard. The technology of preparing various articles and also, the study of their quality strongly interested me. And so, I studied it with zeal. The first part of Karl Marx's "*Kapital*," which we had to go through, I read over in a single breath, lying on my hard bed. The female professor who led the seminar pertaining to this subject heard my prepared lecture with an astonished face and gave me a good grade.

I also liked chemistry very much. Once, I attended a chemistry seminar, even while being sick with jaundice.

Trouble clung to me. On Abramovsky Boulevard, the wheel of a vehicle rode over my previously sick, left foot. I fell down. Two of my girlfriends barely managed to schlep me to the institute. The entire way, I hopped on one foot. It was a miracle that it was not far. They had to cut off the boot because the foot was swollen and blue. For a month I was laid-up with compresses on my foot and ate sugar beets, as a remedy for jaundice. It was a shame about the boots with the thin soles, which I had received as a present from my uncle Dovid. More like these I never again had in the Soviet Union.

As the recipient of a Stalin stipend [scholarship], I needed to be an active *komsomolka*.[44] I helped students prepare their homework and participated in all the cultural events. We ended the school year. Summer. And so, they once again sent us to work in the field, in a sovkhoz,[45] twenty kilometers from the Djuma train station. We tore out the stalks from the soil with our hands because they were lacking the appropriate tools. We would begin working at three o'clock in the morning, so as not to have to work under the scorching sun, by day. They once again gave us to eat the *"zatsheruche"* – the long-known soup of water and gruel, but in addition – a piece of very dark meat.

Two girls developed high fevers. I was the "elder" – the party responsible for the group. So, I decided to take them back home.

---

[44] *Komsomolka* is the female version of *komsomol*, or a member of the Young Communist Union under the Soviet Regime.

[45] A sovkhoz was a state-owned farm of the former Soviet Union, which paid waged to the workers. See: https://www.merriam-webster.com/dictionary/sovkhoz (accessed 6-13-24).

With a wagon we rode to the Djuma train station. Masses of people would besiege every train, and we were unable to push ourselves into a wagon. I was despondent.

A train with petroleum cisterns came to a stop. On a little bridge between the large barrels, I spotted a person. I decided to do the same – to drop down onto the little bridge. The person helped us, stretched out a hand. Along the way, we hugged ourselves together, so as not to fall off. At a station, a train operator spotted us. He demanded one hundred rubles bribe money from us, or else he would throw us off. I gave him the fifty rubles, which I was holding in my passport. But he did not otherwise want to return the passport to me, as collateral that I would give him fifty more rubles. But the unknown man got involved and convinced him to return the document.

When the train slowly rode to the Samarkand depot, we jumped down and hid, so that the train police would not catch us and arrest us. The fifty rubles from my account were gone.

The following day I told the institute that it was impossible to be at that sovkhoz and asked to be sent somewhere else. They sent me to go pick fruit with another group. We took to the fruit, and also enjoyed the small potatoes with butter, which we would get to eat, and thought that we had encountered much good fortune. We, however, did not know that in that area there was a tropical malaria raging. I came home with a high fever.

I grew ill with malaria and in addition, also with dysentery, most likely because of eating unwashed fruit. I was extremely ill. So as to catch a bit of fresh air, they would carry me outside in their arms, to the yard. My Aunt Clara would feed me with the water from the cooked rice and with grated apples. Once, when I was already able to steady myself on my feet and went into the bread shop to purchase the usual bread, the shopkeeper said to me that I should leave as soon as possible, because he was scared of me; that is how terrible I looked...

I was always accustomed to having friends around me, good friends. I loved having someone whisper words of "endearment" in my ear. And so, I befriended a Russian-Jewish student, Volodya – a young, thin fellow with curly hair and a longish face. It really bothered me that during the course of my illness he never came to pay me a convalescent visit. He himself was barely seventeen years old, following a heart attack. His mother was the librarian of the institute. They sent her and her children from Moscow to Samarkand, even before the war, after they arrested her husband, an engineer whom they would earlier on send out of the country to purchase vehicles. Both of them, she, and her husband, were active Communists, and being immersed in work and in social activities, they neglected their home and children. Volodya related to me that while yet in Moscow, he befriended young thieves, and during the night, they would rob stores. His father, following his arrest, no longer saw him again. During the lectures at the institute, we would both sit side-by-side. He would, under the bench, take my arm and caress it. We would normally take strolls and schmooze. Also, we went to the river, a few kilometers beyond the city, to swim.

Suddenly, Volodya vanished.

Sometime later I received a letter from him with claims that I had another boyfriend, who was, according to him, not worth anything; furthermore, he did not come to me. It turned out that they had suddenly mobilized Volodya, and he did not have an opportunity to inform me of this. Volodya's brother, Yuri, a capable engineer, I visited years later in Israel. Volodya and his family remained in the Soviet Union.

At that time, in Samarkand, raged spotted typhus.

Once, while going out to the street, I saw a sick Jew lying on the ground. I took him to the hospital and left behind my address. A few weeks later, he appeared – pale, skinny, with an outstretched nose. He survived the spotted typhus. He complained that he did not have a single groschen to move to a *voyenkomat*, that is, to a mobilization office, and that he was very hungry. I gave away my last five rubles to him, and my last piece of bread – a *lepyoshka*.

Years later we met each other in Israel. His joy was without measure. He now gave me his first name and family name: Abrasha Hirshfeld. He did not know how to thank me for my help back then, which literally saved his life. A short time later he visited me and brought me a present – a self-painted oil painting: a bouquet of flowers.

Jewish Youths from Poland in Samarkand

There was much joy among us: Fimke Goldberg, my cousin, came from the front to convalesce at his parents' home. He was still wounded.

דער קוזין פֿימקע גאָלדבערג

Photograph: My cousin, Fimke Goldberg

Fimke was born in Leningrad and already at the beginning of the war, he willingly signed up for the army. A bullet went through his face. He was terribly starved. He would gladly go to buy the bread with the bread cards, and on the way, he would bite at the bread from all sides.

I was with him in the movie theater and turned down the invitation of Dr. Aminov, who once again tuned up in Samarkand. I simply wanted the wounded soldier to have a bit of enjoyment before he had to return to the front.

Suddenly Fimke developed a high fever, and he shook from ague. He became ill with a severe case of malaria and was laid-up for weeks in the hospital. His parents would sit beside his bed for complete days at a time. When he returned from the hospital, they sold some of their goods in the marketplace and bought food for him, but not too much. They hoped that if he were emaciated, they would not send him back to the front. It, however, did not help. He had to return to the army.

From the second son, Siomke, no news arrived from the front.

I later met with Dr. Aminov. He revealed to me that he had planned and hoped to marry me... Who would have thought?!

The institute at that time consumed the most important place in my life. Here, I befriended many Jewish students, youths from Poland, who grouped themselves in the student residence. There was a soup kitchen there where they would give the students "lunches": a watery soup with broad noodles made of black meal, a few green cabbage leaves, and overcooked kishkes [i.e., intestines/derma]. I relented on the kishkes and gave somebody else another one.

I will mention several of the Jewish students, whom I got to know.

Two fellows from Krakow, Chilek [diminutive for Yechiel] and Heniek, would go about the city with a saw and a hatchet, looking for work. Heniek was dressed in a gymnasium uniform with the red belt of the Polish lyceum; and I would always look at him, even before we got to know each other.

My remarkably familiar student, Chilek, and his brother, lost both of their parents in Samarkand, who, died on the same day here, of typhus.

Arontshik – a tall, handsome fellow, also took up trade. He would carry around small, paper bags with aromatic powder, which one of his relatives had produced.

Regarding Pinek [likely a diminutive for Pinchas], an affable student with a round face and smiling eyes, people would say that he had golden hands. He and another student, Avrahamel, trafficked in bread cards. I encountered them on my way to the barracks while carrying food for my brother, Berele. They asked me not to tell about their activities. In the end, they fled from Samarkand, out of fear that they would be caught speculating with the bread cards.

In order to bring about a particular outcome, nearly all the Jewish students from Poland trafficked in whatever they could. The biggest wheeler-dealer was, it seems to me, Osher. When the Polish assembly point handed out good butter, soap, and other products that the Polish refugees were lacking, Osher distributed this. On his lists were also "dead souls." Even my relatives from Leningrad received a "*pajqk*."[46] He and his friend, Fredek, pushed two boxes of soap under my bed. The soap stank and bothered me terribly when I had an attack of malaria.

---

[46] In Polish, this word can mean "lamp," "light fixture," or "chandelier." It is not clear if this is meant to be taken literally here. More likely, it connotes some sort of designated quantity of living necessities.

Map of Uzbekistan and Neighboring Countries from the
University of Texas at Austin, Perry-Castañeda Library (PCL)
Map Collection[47]

---

[47] See:
https://maps.lib.utexas.edu/maps/commonwealth/uzbekistan_rel94.jpg (accessed 6-25-24).

These two fellows also got out of the train heading for Tashkent, to barter with manufactured goods. Stuffed with linen under their clothes, they stood an entire night on the wagon stairs. It was extremely dangerous.

There was an instance when they traveled to Ashgabat,[48] ostensibly, to recruit students for our institute. En route, on the way, Osher lost his money and documents. It flew out through the open window of the train, when he climbed up to a higher wooden cot. Both of the friends stopped the train, got out, and searched for the lost items. But fruitlessly. With heartache they traveled onward. It did not disturb them to do business with a watchmaker from Ashgabat who gave them a stunning brooch with huge diamonds and emeralds for "somebody." It did not occur to them to flee with the valuable merchandise. Factually, they never would have submitted to such a thing. They looked after the merchant's daughter, Sara, who rode with them to Samarkand and registered for our institute.

One could accomplish the best trafficking while recruiting students, because one was traveling around with official documents across various cities. The professors assisted in the recruitment work because they were interested in having as many students as possible.

In my courses there were a lot of Korean students, and also local residents and refugees from Russia, White Russia, the Ukraine, Lithuania, Latvia, and Estonia. In general, everybody took their studies seriously.

The student, Zshenia [Genia], was a unique type – a tall girl with flickering gold hair twisted around hair tubes.

---

[48] Ashgabat is the capital and largest city of Turkmenistan.

She was a leader in the Komsomol. She even sold the organization's used newspapers at the marketplace. Her parents – her mother, a doctor, her father, an economist – were mobilized, and they were on the front. From there, they would send her packages with all sorts of goodies. My aunt prompted her that she should give me some sort of present from her goodies, because I helped her prepare for the exams. She, however, ignored this. The dean promised her parents that he would take it upon himself to assist her. So, she told me that he indeed, "took it upon" himself in a special manner... Also, a fellow courted her, used her: she fed him, clothed him, and after that, he left her.

There was a female student from Smolensk, Natasha, whom a couple from Samarkand, doctors, adopted. For breakfast, she would eat a white roll with butter and cocoa. Oh, was I jealous of her!

The group of students from Poland would meet each other from time to time. For my girlfriend, Janka's voluntary departure to the front with the Polish military, we took a photograph. She fell on the front.

We had a very good time New Year's Eve at the home of the student, Liza. She informed us that this was her wedding celebration; she married the student of agronomy, Yechezkel.

Also, Sarale, a student of medicine, and Heniek, a veterinary student, were my friends.

To this very group of students belonged Fredek, a student of economics, strategic planning, and statistics, at our institute. I got to know him by chance when he sat next to me one evening at the anniversary celebration of the October Revolution. I looked at the Polish newspaper that was in his hands. My name was called to receive an accolade. This intrigued him. My name was familiar to him. It came out that he knew my father from Chelyabinsk. Later on, he told me that he fled from Chelyabinsk, in order to be mobilized in the Polish Army of General Anders. They, however, did not accept him, because they did not need any Jews.

And so, we got to know Fredek. My aunt invited him to our home for the Passover Seder. He brought several bottles of good Uzbek wine – Porto, Topaz, and Muscat. My aunt went out to take a walk with him and questioned him whether he had a wife and children somewhere.

It came out that he was a solitary young man. His parents sent him away from home when the Germans began to grab youths to perform unskilled labor. He left to illegally cross the border with several other Jews. A German detained them but let them go. And they came across to the Soviet side. Having a Matura, Fredek found work as a teacher in Luck [pronounced `Lutsk']. After Hitler befell the Soviet Union, Fredek went on foot and by train to reach Samarkand.

His officer's boots, which he had from home, came in useful along the difficult road. But not for long did he enjoy them. In Samarkand's large city bath house, on one particular day, he left behind his things, as always, in a cabinet. The boots somebody "exchanged" for a pair of old slippers... He sold his watch, and for the money, he purchased a pair of shoes at the marketplace. It turned out, though, that those were two left shoes...

My aunt's Uzbek acquaintance whom she "smeared" [i.e., bribed], so that he not bother us, not steal from us, persuaded Fredek that he would buy him shoes at "Voyentorg" – a store for officers. He came in with the money through one door and exited through another... The shoes he did, indeed, purchase, but both the shoes, as well as the money, fell by the wayside. Fredek related the story to me later on, once he already finally had heavy, black shoes on his feet.

When Fredek came to Samarkand, he registered at our institute and came to live in the student residence. In order to have something on which to subsist, he would from time-to-time traffic in whatever it may be, although this smelled of risk. There was, however, no choice.

The first evening, at the October celebration, while we got to know each other by chance, Fredek followed after me, step by step. He invited me to dance and would not allow anyone else to approach me. At the lottery, we won a small plaster picture and a bottle of wine. He accompanied me home in the Old Town, and when saying goodbye, gave me a kiss. From then on, he was a frequent guest by us. He was dressed in a long, green overcoat, or in the dark blue suit, still from home.

Fredek was thin. A good smile rested upon his totally pale lips. His beautiful eyes were often red from inflammation. In his pocket he always carried a large knife, to have something to defend himself with. It was dangerous at night to walk alone across the city. They used to assault people, made them get undressed naked, literally naked, and took their things. One thanked God that they allowed one to live. It was a life threat to meet up with the Samarkand underworld. The truth is that it was not very pleasant to show up stark naked in the student residence...

The first time Fredek invited me to the movie theater, he treated me with a candy. The second time – with a slice of bread and butter – both hard to come by. We ate this and drank it down with chicory coffee at a small table at the marketplace.

The marketplace was full of people. The refugees would sell their clothes and other desirables there. The most successful among the Russians and Uzbeks were the Polish watches. They would wear several watches on one arm. I cannot forget a scene at the marketplace, when my father bent over, over a sack of vegetables, to select something for himself. An Uzbek rolled up his coat and pushed his hand into a pocket, with the clear intent of pulling something out of there. When my father hastily stood up and looked at the pickpocket in amazement, the fellow began to beat him up, like some would say, because he would not allow himself to be robbed...

I Get Married

Fredek told me that he was already 26 years old, and it was time for him to get married. Furthermore, he was asking for my hand... For me, in the meantime, it did not even enter my mind. I was young, incredibly young. I thought only about studying, completing my studies at the institute. Gradually, he convinced me that yes, I should marry him. He was very dear to me, worrying about me. During my frequent attacks of malaria, he would take me to the doctor to get the injections against the sickness. I was so weak that alone, to the doctor, I simply would not walk. Not only walking, but even sitting was difficult, being so full of shots from the injections. It did not bother Fredek that following all these difficult illnesses I remained without hair on my head, and furthermore, always wore a black beret in the street, among people.

Incidentally, Fredek walked with me, 16 kilometers on foot, back and forth, when Berele's regiment departed for the front, and we said farewell to him for good.

Gradually, the hairs began to grow in, and for my wedding, I already had short hair. One could not think about a wedding dress. From an old American, dark blue coat, they sewed me a "new" dress. I received blue shoes, old and a bit crooked, from the Polish Punkt, where they distributed old American goods.

עס זיצן: דוד און קלאַראַ גאָלדבערג; עס שטייען: די אויטאָרין און פרעדעק

Photograph: Sitting: Dovid and Clara Goldberg; standing: the authoress and Fredek

Osher was the witness when we registered at the local office, "Zags." In "Torgsin" – a store for foreigners – Fredek bought two gold rings. In the evening, for the wedding, ten people gathered together in our kibitka: friends, several neighbors, my aunt and uncle and the landlord, the Uzbek. My aunt prepared gefilte fish and strudel, cooked and baked on a kerosene stove. We drank wine. I drank up a vial – a bowl – of strong, thick Uzbek wine, and became drunk. Tipsily, I walked with my husband into his room on Lenin Street in the New Town.

Into our new residence we took in my aunt and uncle. We brought in two beds, a table and stools, my aunt's sewing machine, and a small table with the kerosene lamp for cooking. There was no washroom in the home, it is understood, and we would go in a booth in the yard [i.e., an outhouse?]. We all, together, rented the place of residence. It did not cost us little. The previously large room was subdivided by a small plywood partition. In the other half lived a professor, Dr. Turkiewicz, and his young wife, also a doctor, and their young son. Young students would come to her, and it was lively there… Her husband was often drunk, such that we did not have any rest from the neighbors.

At that time, my scholarship increased to 700 rubles, and I gave it away to my aunt, who tended to the household duties for all four of us.

Time flew by. The difficult war years were nearing an end. With joy we heard the radio speaker, the Jew, Yuri Levitan, who jubilantly let it be known that the Red Army was progressing and liberating completely new cities and areas; that finally, the second front had been opened. The names of the liberated cities in Poland stirred up our longing for home.

The 8th of May 1945, when Germany capitulated, people danced in the streets, and also us Jews, in the celebratory world. Along with the neighbors we drank "L'Chaim." Difficult to describe the exalted mood: the end of the terrible war, goodbye!

Almost no one knew precisely what had happened in Poland and in Europe, in general. And of course, we did not know how great was the woe of our people. Fredek sent a letter to his parents in his Polish hometown.

And a reply arrived from the Magistrate that his family was not here, and that there were no remaining Jews in the town. Fredek cried bitterly. How his own perished, he only first learned, later on: his father died in the Warsaw Ghetto; his youngest sister was taken, downtrodden and apathetic, to the ovens of Auschwitz; his mother, a sister, and brother were taken with the death transports. Even earlier on, before Fredek fled from Poland, one of his sisters was killed before his eyes, in a line for bread, during the bombings of Warsaw. This was the sum total of his family, and that meant that he remained all alone... I tried to console him, although tears also ran by me [i.e., from my own eyes], and my heart was choked-up.

Now, we saw that thanks to our having fled from our homes, we saved ourselves from a certain death. Yes, we had luck. Could one compare our difficulties during the evacuation and the suffering we experienced as refugees in foreign places with the fate of the Jews who fell into the Nazi plight?

And now, following the war? None of us, the war refugees, wanted to remain in Middle Asia. Our being here we considered only a temporary stage and hoped to return to Poland. We, indeed, did not know, and perhaps did not wish to believe at all, that everything in our old home had disappeared, away with the smoke; that the old home no longer existed at all.

During summer vacation, just after the war, I went to Chelyabinsk, to my parents and Leizerke.

The journey from Samarkand to Chelyabinsk on the Ural Mountains, by train, lasted several long days. Initially, we stayed over in Tashkent at Vove's place. He relinquished his bed to me and fed me with roasted meat and tasty vegetables. Until late in the night we schmoozed and recalled our home in Bereza. He had not had any news regarding his family and was very anxious. There was reason to consider the worst because appalling news was heard from all sides. Another night along the way, while switching to another train, a passenger, a Polish Jew, took us in to his [or her?] residence, where we were able to straighten out our bones upon the floor. However, so many bedbugs attacked me there that I had to strain myself that night on a table.

I traveled to Chelyabinsk on the very top shelf of the wagon, which actually looked like baggage. I held fast to my suitcase, so that nobody would steal it from me during the night. The robberies in the wagons and at the depots were terrible.

At the stations and along the road, peasant women sold fish and dried fruit. They also bartered salt and flour, along with tea and raisins.

Exhausted, but fortunate, I ultimately reached my own. My father and mother were commandants of the barracks where mobilized workers lived, and there was a room with beds for themselves and for Leizerke, as well as enough food.

It was very pleasant to be with my family for a stretch of time. I got to know the city a bit. Chelyabinsk is a big industrial city with a lot of schools of higher education and a university. I specially went to the medical institute, so as to locate a Jewish student, Boris, whose cousin was with us in Samarkand and asked me to give him his regards. Boris did not know that his relative had managed to flee from the Germans and save himself. Given that the cousin had, for certain reasons, changed his family name, he had not written to Boris, and asked that I put the two of them in contact. And that, it is understood, I did.

With Boris, now a doctor in Hadera, I have been friendly for over forty years.

Riding back from Chelyabinsk to Samarkand, I, quick as a landowner's wife, entered the salon wagon. Following all of those freight wagons in which I wandered about across Russia, this was a huge luxury. Modestly furnished, but clean and quiet – a pleasure! How did I come to be there? In the train, I by chance encountered a friend of mine from the institute. Her stepfather was the chief of the train, and he prepared it so nicely for us. The best thing was that he provided each of us with a separate compartment. We, however, wanted to ride together, and schmoozed late into the night. We did not notice how in the morning, we had reached Samarkand, and how they had placed us on another train line following our arrival.

Fredek waited for me, but did not find me, and returned home disappointed. How great was his joy when I arrived, a while later. Fredek had managed to acquire a lot of Jewish acquaintances in the city, and he negotiated with them about whatever he was able. All the students needed to find a livelihood. The majority did not have a relative, or a savior who would support them in their studies. And so, they needed to support themselves. And primarily, through trafficking, although this was risky enough. If one were caught, one would be harshly prosecuted for "speculation."

To what degree the wheeling-dealing, and even the traveling around was tied up in true life risks, Arontshik's case may serve as an example. He would earn a living by transporting trucks with raisins from a kolkhoz all the way to the factory. Once, he was shown a receipt with his signature for five tons of raisins, which had not arrived at the factory. He looked at the piece of paper at the window, in good lighting, and noticed that his signature had been fabricated, copied beneath carbon copy paper. He grew very afraid – he could be arrested for theft.

So, he consulted the professor of jurisprudence. He advised him to disappear as quickly as possible from the city, because he would not have any great chances of showing his innocence. So, he did, indeed, decide, along with Chilek, not to wait long, and leave for Lemberg.

Chilek was also anxious. With him, the following took place: while chopping and sawing wood, he fell into a ditch and injured one of his feet. So, he would go around with a fat stick, hobbling. One night, a hooligan assaulted him, wanted to take off his clothes. And so, with the stick, he gave the assaulter such a whack on the head that he fell over and remained lying. Chilek hastily fled from that site, and the entire time contemplated: who knows how hard he hit the person? And so, he, too, needed to disappear from Samarkand.

At that time, a group of Jews assembled, and through various combinations, wrenched themselves out of Middle Asia and returned to Europe.

Of our friends, Polish Jews, the first ones went to Lemberg – Moniek, Yosef and his girlfriend, Galia, and her mother, yellow Tonye [Tanya?], Chilek, and Arontshik. The student, Yossel S., had some money on him, and our friends hoped that he would help them out along the way. They hoped in vain. Along the way, the company was hungry, but they overcame all the difficulties.

When we learned of this, we, too, decided to leave Uzbekistan. It was not an easy thing. Without a *"propsuk,"* that is, a special permit, one could not get a ticket for the train. And so, it occurred to me to request a permit to travel to my hometown of Bereza; and we obtained the *"propsuk."*

With heart pangs we said goodbye to my aunt and uncle, who already planned to return to Leningrad, their permanent place of residence. They still hoped to find their son, Siome, a seaman of the naval fleet. Somebody told them that he was spotted in Leningrad. They, however, did not find him. He fell in the war. Their residence in the old count's house with the mirrors and the marble steps waited for them; everything, aside from one room, which had been allocated for a war invalid.

From Leningrad they wrote me that my grandmother and grandfather had died during the siege of the city. My aunt and uncle never complained that it was difficult for them. I, however, knew that they needed help, and sent them packages with a few rubles from every place where I happened to be – whether through the mail, or through other means. They died at the age of approximately seventy. They did not have an easy life.

My Aunt Clara and Uncle Dovid were like a father and mother to me. We helped one another during the bitter-hard war years. One thing is certain; that were it not for my scholarship, we would all have suffered from hunger and want.

Their son, and my cousin, Fimke, returned from the front. Initially, to Leningrad. He, however, crossed over to Riga, Latvia, where he raised a family. I corresponded with him for a long time and sent him presents: clothing, shoes. A few years later he died in an automobile accident.

The war had ended. People were moving from there. We, too, went on our way.

With a heavy heart, but with a feeling of hope for a better tomorrow, we said farewell to our friends, acquaintances, and professors from the institute. It appeared that people were envious of us. Sometime later, the general, organized repatriation of the former Polish citizens back to Poland, took place.

Our return trip was more difficult.

We packed up our small number of things, our bedding, and several kilograms of raisins, and sent them according to the train ticket, to Kartuz-Bereza. We sat down at the depot, waiting for the train. Trains are trains; we had tickets, and indeed, could not push ourselves into a wagon. Speculators besieged the trains en masse, and they were the travelers. In the end, it worked out for us. A train with a freight wagon that was traveling to Moscow, stopped. For weeks, we schlepped ourselves in this, across the Soviet Union. We stood, more than rode. The large wagon was packed full of people, mostly Jews. We grabbed a place on a wooden cot. So that it would not be so hard to lie down, we placed my new coat under us.

In the congestion of people, unwashed, lice befell us, which crawled from one to the other. When we finally reached Moscow, the first problem was – to bathe ourselves in a city bath house, where we could also disinfect our things. Doing this, we looked for a friend of ours from Samarkand, Rubina, and by her we stayed the first night. By day we went to view the city. I was delighted by the subway – the metro – whose stunning stations with the multi-colored marble walls with the mosaic ornaments and pictures, with the metal decorations and large lamps – were similar to palaces. We strolled across the beautiful streets, across the park, and marveled at the little shop and the colorful church council with the "onion cupolas," which stood next door.

Two days we stood in line for tickets to travel further. The third night, I was the first at the cashier window. Everyone was pushing, practically thrusting me aside. With my last bit of strength, I held fast to the window and barely managed to convince the cashier that the *"propsuk"* for travel to Bereza was in the direction to Lvov (Lemberg), due to the fact that Bereza is next to the city, and to get there, we would travel on foot... In the end, the cashier sold us tickets to Lvov – Lemberg.

Our baggage was sent off, according to the submitted address in Bereza...

In Lemberg

We decided to go to Lemberg, because there we had somewhere to study further and complete our high school education. Our friends, friends from the Samarkand institute with whom we established somewhat of a letter correspondence, also lived there. We rode in the direction of Kiev. One wagon window was open. It was blowing into the wagon and a girl blocked the window with her suitcase. Suddenly, the suitcase disappeared. Thieves moved about on the rooftops of the wagons; they were looking for a "livelihood" and were responsible for this act. The robbed girl, understandably, cried bitterly about her loss. Everyone had been impoverished by the war, and every little bit of property was valuable.

We arrived in Lemberg and only then did we see the ruined depot. Individual houses and also entire quarters had been destroyed. The streets still carried Polish names, and everywhere – monuments for Polish poets and fighters. The opera and the theater – in the center of the city. The marketplace, where people would sell off their goods so as to have sustenance, was extremely close. Only at the marketplace could one freely buy food: bread, baked goods, meat, and sausages. A truly postwar mood.

For the first time, I traveled by streetcar. Somebody asked me: What time is it? I looked at my hand and noticed that little by little, I was losing my watch because a thief had undone the strap.

We had the address of our friends. We arrived there, saw that they lived in a large, empty room with a partially fallen-in tile oven, without water, and without sanitary comforts. We no longer encountered our friends here. At the first opportunity, they left for Poland, rushed back home... In the room remained the yellow Tonye [or Tanya?] and Galia and her mother, who left Samarkand, who left their former hometown in order to live in Europe under new conditions.

We took advantage of the mattresses that our friends left behind and slept on them on the floor. There was no furniture in the room. On the eastern wall hung, unclear for what purpose, a lone wooden spoon... Tonye related how Chilek would pray to the wooden spoon. The Polish neighbor got along very well with us. She would sometimes cook or bake us something.

In Lemberg we by chance encountered Sara and her sister – the daughters of the watchmaker and jewelry dealer from Ashgabat. They had *protektsye* [i.e., special connections] to get a place of residence. And so, they also helped us, and we moved into a furnished room at the home of an old Polish woman. Here, we were able to use the kitchen and the bathroom. Our little bit of bedding and the ten kilos of raisins that we had sent as "baggage," arrived in Bereza. We were very much lacking bedding. Instead of a sheet, until we received our packed goods, we slept on a rag.

Fredek became acquainted with Lemberg Jews and bartered with them. From one of them, he purchased, to another, he sold.

From a soldier in the marketplace, he purchased a cheap ring with a diamond, and I wore this for many years.

At the marketplace one could purchase all sorts of goods, even chickens. The old female Pole taught me how to pluck the feathers from a chicken, how one removes the intestines.

Here, in Lemberg, we truly lived it up. We would often go to the opera and see the most beautiful operas, operettas, and ballets. In the theater halls we heard Russians saying: "What? The `French' have once again gathered together?" – meaning the Jews...

I registered for a trade institute whose department was that of commodities/marketing. The dean was a Pole. The building had previously belonged to the trade academy in Lvov (Lemberg). Given that the city had been incorporated within the borders of the Ukraine, studies at the institute were conducted in Russian and also in Ukrainian, and I needed, as quickly as possible, to master Ukrainian and pass the language exams.

I was sent for an internship to a large store, "Univermag," and to a leather factory. Indeed, I wrote my diploma work about leather. The diploma exams took place straightforwardly.

I still see before my eyes the large, packed room of students, the stage with the examiners' committee, which consisted of Muscovite professors who had been sent down. We submitted the diploma exams after pulling out a page of questions. I responded tersely and sharply, although with my beating heart I had had enough.

Ultimately, I completed my studies and received a diploma. I was advised to remain as an assistant at the institute. I turned this down with the excuse that we would, it appeared, be leaving here, possibly for Palestine.

At the graduation celebration at the institute, we had an exceptionally good time – danced, sang. I felt like a new period in my life was beginning.

My father came to us from Chelyabinsk for a few weeks. He also went to Bereza and sent us the baggage. From Bereza he arrived, totally broken. I noticed that he had literally grown grey. He went about depressed and silent and did not want to relate what he had seen in Bereza. Gradually, he began to open up: part of the town had been burnt – the houses to one side of the avenue and the marketplace were no longer there. After the Germans had set fire to the stunning Kadisha house of religious study, the fire spread across the town and consumed the small wooden houses.

There was no remaining memory of ghetto "A" in a few streets for "useful" Jews, and ghetto "B," for the "not-useful" Jews. Beneath the green trees of Bereza there were no more Moysheles or Shloymeles.[49] Not a Yiddish word, no Jewish prayer in a house of religious study, or at the cemetery – one no longer hears this... My father learned of the horrifying burial grounds in the forest, Bronna-Góra, and also, in the forest where we used to get together on Lag Ba'Omer with our school, in the bosom of nature. Now, those same trees hover silently over the mass graves of the Bereza grandfathers and grandmothers, of fathers and mothers, of the yet living ebullient youths and sweet little children whom the Nazis shot in October 1942, after having tortured them for a year, behind the ghetto fences.

---

[49] This is an allusion to the Yiddish poem, "Under the Green Little Trees" written by Chaim Nachman Bialik, but later adapted during the Holocaust to reflect that there were [virtually] no more Moysheles and Shloymeles, in light of this great Jewish catastrophe.

מ. בערנשטיין: "יזכּור"

M. Bernstein: "Yizkor"

My father moved about over the ruins of his former home where he was born, raised, got married, raised a family, and led a not easy, honest life. From our home there only remained the brick floor – a grey, cement spot – as a silent headstone...

Other details about the destruction of Bereza's Jews I heard from my friend, the former partisan, Moyshe Tuchman. He fled from the ghetto, hid, and fought against the Germans as a partisan in the woods of Polesia. Along with Russians, White Russians, the Jewish partisans, derailed German trains, killed Nazi occupants, at every possible opportunity. The partisans suffered from the rain and ice, from mud, and snow, from hunger and sickness – and endured! Moyshe told me that for the murder in Bronna-Góra, the Jews of Bereza were taken by train – they were driven into the wagons from one side and pushed out from the other side – directly into the prepared graves, where they shot them, en masse.[50] Empty wagons with the clothing of the martyrs returned to Bludnye, the Bereza train station... Individuals saved themselves from the graves. A young woman with a little child in her arms, who were not hit by the bullets, crept out of the grave in the middle of the night.

Even before the total liquidation of the ghetto, people here committed suicide and did not wait until the Germans would murder them. The harness-maker hanged his children and afterward – himself. The teacher, Rochel Chmiel-Shapiro, together with Ciankali [sp.?], poisoned her child, her husband, and herself.

They also tried to stage an uprising; dug a tunnel so as to be able to flee from the ghetto during a time of trouble, but without success. People suffocated inside of it from smoke while Bereza burned.

---

[50] For more historical context about the mass killing of Jews from Bereza Kartuska at the Bronna-Góra railway station, as well as contemporary images of the former killing site, see: https://collections.yadvashem.org/en/untold-stories/killing-site/14627257-Bronna-Gora-Railway-Station-Area (accessed 4-13-24).

Individuals left for Pruzhany, which was incorporated into the Third Reich. In vain, they hoped to save themselves there.

Near the ruins of the Kartuz monastery, the Germans shot the Poles at whose homes they uncovered hidden Jews. That was the town pharmacist at whose home they found Leitshe Kasierski, one of the prettiest girls in town. Here, the entire family of Chorew's son was shot for hiding Taibele Kaplan. The fate of the Jewish girls who tried to save their lives is evident...

Several Jewish boys from Bereza managed to flee to the woods. Several evacuated themselves to the Soviet Union, and in this manner, saved themselves. My family was from these fortunate ones, although we, too, paid a dear price – Berele, who fell in battle with the Nazi-Germans.

My parents merited dying in Israel, at the age of eighty-something years. They departed the world with a clear understanding; they did not become a burden to anyone; they worked until the last minute in their store, together with my brother, Leizer, and my son, Benny. The double headstone of my father and mother stands in the cemetery in Kiryat-Shaul, Tel-Aviv.

דער פּאַרטיזאַן משה טוכמאַן

The partisan, Moyshe Tuchman

We, the surviving Jews from Bereza in Israel and elsewhere, erected a headstone for our town a few years ago in the cemetery in Holon, in Israel.

With my memories, I also had the intention of erecting a certain headstone for our hometown and for Jewish life in it.

While describing Bereza and Jewish life in the town, aside from my memory, I was also aided by the *"Pinkes fun finf fartilikte kehiles – Pruzshene, Bereze, Maltsh, Shereshev un Selts – zeyer oyfkum, geshichte un umkum"* ["Record Book of the Five Annihilated Jewish Communities – Pruzhany, Bereza, Malcz, Szereszów and Selets] – Their Rise, History and Destruction"]. The "Record Book" was published in Buenos Aires in 1958. For the fifteenth anniversary following their cruel liquidation. Editor – Mordechai V. Bernstein. This book was published by the *landsleit* [i.e., kinsmen] associations of the above-mentioned towns in Argentina, with the co-partnership of the *landsleit* in Israel, United States of America, and Canada.[51]

And may I be permitted to mention the names of the departed, well-known *landsleit* of our unforgettable hometown, Bereza, personalities of which we may be proud. Those are –

The well-known Yiddish writer, Kadya Molodowsky,[52] in her youth, was a friend of my mother. Jewish children throughout the world recited her popular children's songs and poems.

---

[51] For further bibliographic details about this memorial book, see: https://search.worldcat.org/title/13306395 (accessed 4-13-24).

[52] Further biographical details about Kadya Molodowsky (1894-1975) may be found at the following links:
https://jwa.org/encyclopedia/article/molodowsky-kadya;
https://congressforjewishculture.org/people/3120/Molodovski,%20K adye%20(May%2010,%201894%E2%80%93March%2023,%201975)
(accessed 4-13-24).

The well-known Hebrew poet, Dov Chomsky;[53] the poetess Masha Shtuker-Paiuk.[54] She wrote for children and adults, and also authored a larger poem about our hometown;[55]

The world-renowned Rabbi Yitzchak-Elchanan Spektor O"BM,[56] in his youth, was a rabbi in Bereza. In his name, there are streets in several cities and a neighborhood in Tel-Aviv, Nahalat Yitzhak;

My uncle, the Yiddish writer, Yosl Babitsh, who lived in Pruzhany. He published in the Warsaw "Haynt" ["Today"], "Moment," "Literarishe Bleter" ["Literary Pages"], [and] the New York "Morgn Zshurnal" ["Morning Journal"]. He perished in the Pruzhany Ghetto, 1942;

May he be distinguished for long life [i.e., the following individual was still alive when the author wrote her autobiography] – Leizer Abramowicz, the commander of a partisan camp. He served in

---

[53] For further information about Dov Chomsky (1913-1976), a Hebrew poet and educator, see:
https://www.jewishvirtuallibrary.org/chomsky-dov (accessed 4-13-24).

[54] Additional biographical details about Masha Shtuker-Paiuk (1914-1988) may be found at the following links:
https://shevazucker.com/40-masha-shtuker-paiuk-im-becoming-my-mother/; https://congressforjewishculture.org/people/2207/Shtuker-Payuk,%20Mashe%20(October%205,%201914%E2%80%931988) (accessed 4-13-24).

[55] The poem to which the author alludes here appears to be the one that appears in English translation at the following link:
https://www.jewishgen.org/yizkor/bereza93/ber179.html#Page206 (accessed 4-13-24).

[56] For additional biographical information about Rabbi Spektor, see for instance:
https://yivoencyclopedia.org/article.aspx/Spektor_Yitshak_Elhanan (accessed 4-13-24).

the diplomatic service of postwar Poland in America, China, [and] Turkey;

משה בערנשטיין

Photograph: Moyshe Bernstein

And may he be distinguished for long life – the painter and poet, Moyshele Bernstein, whom I already mentioned in the beginning of my memoirs. He is famous for his graphic works, black and white and colorful paintings, whose central theme is the destroyed Jewish shtetl in Eastern Europe.

Back on Polish Soil

Factually, we no longer had anything to do in Lemberg. Fredek learned that his acquaintances were going to Poland and that there was a special committee that concerned itself with the repatriation of former Polish citizens. I wrote to my parents in Chelyabinsk that we were intending to go to Poland. That is to say, to return home. Home?

The majority of my youth had been spent during the difficult war years. Those were years of hunger, illnesses, and homelessness, years of fear regarding the war's outcome, and concerning the outcome of us, Jews; years of constant struggle for day-to-day existence and exertion to overcome various difficulties. It appeared that I, personally, won this struggle, thanks to a strong will, initiative, optimism, and... a bit of luck.

The old landlady heartily bid us farewell and gave us a present – sewn napkins. She had seen how we would place a tablecloth on the table to eat, even then, when there was no sheet on the bed. I selected from my bundle of books and notebooks those materials, which would perhaps come in useful to me in my future work. We packed our small amount of belongings, we said our goodbyes to our good friends and comrades, and went to the train, which was going westward.

There were many Polish Jews here, in the train. One could hear the Polish language. We passed small towns with the familiar Polish landscape: green fields, rivers, forests, small houses with straw or shingles. Peasants, priests, nuns – already long unseen. Children with the Maciejówka hats with the glossy visor. Yes, I recognize it – we are on Polish ground.

With a choked-up heart, we ride across the Polish soil. We do not see any Jews. We, however, were still unable to accept the terrifying Holocaust that we, Jews, had encountered. Gradually, we understood: millions of Jews disappeared. The small Jewish towns were erased from the surface and would never be resurrected. A period in our Jewish history had vanished – forever.

Who would we, nevertheless, encounter? Would we see familiar Jewish figures? The full cities, the full streets of people were for us, Jews, a desert, empty… The emptiness enveloped with a mourning shawl – the Polish soil – the burial grounds of Polish Jewry. Only numbered Jews appeared in Poland following the war – rescued embers of the enormous conflagration. The Poles wondered: What, again, the Jews? Where did they come from? Did they then not liquidate all of them? Who needs them?

The animalistic anti-Semites could not bear the fact that here and there, returning Jews were showing up. They were raging, the Polish murderers: Jews were yanked with force out of the trains and murdered on the spot. In Kielce there was a mass murder of Jews, who had avoided the Nazi slaughtering knife.[57] This agitated the Jewish world. A shudder enveloped the Jews who had hidden in all sorts of holes, who had survived the death camps, as well as the first Jews who had returned from the Soviet Union – they were in real life danger following their liberation from the Nazi hangmen.

God, God! Why are we so punished? I thought to myself. Why are we not meant to live out our years like all nations of the world? And these remarkably simple, elementary questions exhausted me, did not allow for sleep.

---

[57] This is a reference to the Kielce Pogrom of July 4, 1946, during which local Poles murdered and maimed over forty Jews. For further information about this horrific event, refer to: Joanna Tokarska-Bakir, *Cursed: A Social Portrait of the Kielce Pogrom* (Cornell University Press, November 2023); https://encyclopedia.ushmm.org/content/en/article/the-kielce-pogrom-a-blood-libel-massacre-of-holocaust-survivors (accessed 6-22-24).

Few Jews returned to their hometowns because their homes no longer existed. It was difficult to see foreign people, very often enemies, living in your homes, on your furniture, and using your vessels, and benefiting from your belongings. In the large cities this was not felt so strongly as in the small towns. And so the rescued Jews settled in Lodz [Łódź], Warsaw, Lublin, and other larger cities, and began life anew. In Lower Silesia there was a population growth. In the territories that Poland had received from Germany, Poles settled and also Jews from the Ukraine and White Russia, who had formerly been Polish citizens. They quartered themselves in the empty houses where Germans who had left for Germany with the fleeing German Army, had resided.

Our train of repatriates was sent to Lower Silesia, to a small town, Świdnica. They brought us to a school building. There were already a lot of Jews in the classes. For each one, a small bed had been prepared. People became acquainted, one with the other, and for many hours, sat and related their experiences during the war.

One went in search of work, or simply, to earn some business. We were all repatriates – refugees, who had returned to the country where we had been born and raised. Our home, however, no longer existed and nobody was waiting for us.

We searched for relatives, with the hope that perhaps somebody from the family had survived. People registered their names on lists, which were affixed to the walls of the newly created Jewish institutions in the religious houses of study. Thanks to these very lists, relatives and acquaintances were, indeed, located – a father found his daughter, a man – his wife.

A large portion of the Jews here knew, felt, that the wandering had not yet ended. One ultimately aspired to settle on one's own soil, in one's own land, and become a nation equal to other nations.

There were also those who longed for a bit of family – searched for brothers and sisters, cousins, uncles and aunts in America, Canada, South Africa, and Australia. A lot of them did, indeed, locate relatives, and patiently awaited the immigration requirement, to receive a ship's passenger ticket.

Prewar Communists, idealists, or simply careerists, registered themselves with the Polish Communist Party. They received good positions with a good salary, received good housing, and led a normal life.

Factually, all Jews here led a more or less normal life – whether sitting on the suitcases, or not. One worked in government agencies, in factories and workshops, opened stores in various lines of business, and also bartered silver, gold, and jewelry.

The "TOZ"[58] opened clinics, in which Jewish doctors and nurses worked. The few surviving lawyers also found work to do.

When the Jews showed up in Poland, somebody needed to take up their cause. And so, the Jewish Committee was created. The concept to create this arose in Moscow, even before Poland had been liberated. It was best to establish it in Lublin, where the commissar for Jewish interests was the Bundist, Dr. Hirszhorn.

The Central Committee of the Jews in Poland[59] was established in Warsaw. Its chairman was the former Sejm deputy and leader

---

[58] For information about this Jewish organization that focused on medical welfare, see: https://yivoencyclopedia.org/article.aspx/TOZ (accessed 6-22-24).

[59] For further details regarding the Central Committee of the Jews in Poland—otherwise known as CKŻP, in Polish—see:

of the General Zionists, Dr. Emil Sommerstein, his secretary – the Communist, Pawel Zelicki. In the Committee were representatives of other parties, excepting the Revisionists and the "Agudah."

The government supported the Jews. The primary aid was, however, from the American "Joint."[60] They organized children's homes for orphans, for children who had been hidden among Poles and in the churches. The Jewish children began to learn in Yiddish and in Hebrew schools, conducted, it is understood, by Jewish teachers.

In the larger cities Jewish clubs were organized, to which people would come from Warsaw and from outside of the country, distinguished personalities, writers with talks and lectures. Mourning ceremonies would take place; celebrations were devoted to big events in the history of our people and of Israel.

My husband found out that several of his acquaintances were in a small town, Reichenbach, not far from Świdnica, in Lower Silesia.[61] The name Reichenbach was later changed to Richbach, and afterward, to Dzierżoniów. We relocated there. And we did not have any regrets. The Jews there were resettled in the empty

---

https://yivoencyclopedia.org/article.aspx/Central_Committee_of_Jews_in_Poland (accessed 6-22-24).

[60] For additional historical context regarding the "Joint," otherwise known as the American Jewish Joint Distribution Committee or the JDC, see:
https://yivoencyclopedia.org/article.aspx/American_Jewish_Joint_Distribution_Committee (accessed 6-22-24).

[61] For further information about the settlement of Jews in post-World War II Lower Silesia—particularly in Reichenbach—see: Robert L. Cohn, "Israel in Poland: A Forgotten Moment in Postwar History," *European Judaism: A Journal for the New Europe*, Vol. 44, No. 2 (Autumn 2011): 70-80.

houses, which the Germans had abandoned. Most of the time these were brick, small houses, with pointed roofs; narrow streets, paved with large, flat stones. An avenue surrounded the city. In the middle was a marketplace with stores, which Jews also opened.

I recall a Jewish saleswoman with a cross on her throat. She was still afraid, did not want anyone to know about her origins.

There were Jews who once again spoke Yiddish, also on the street. Among us Jews it was a bit homier [i.e., speaking Yiddish] in this foreign environment.

In our city, several kibbutzim of young people who were preparing themselves to go to Israel were established.

In the local hospital, the first postwar Jewish children were born. Rumors circulated that a German nurse was injecting poison into the children's heads, and that the children would die immediately after having been born.

In the opened Jewish cooperatives worked tailors and shoemakers. There were even Jewish coal miners present.

We moved into a small apartment with two rooms. We did not find any German belongings, but bedbugs were not lacking there.

אין דזשערדזשאַניוו, פֿון רעכטס: ניאָמע קאַגאַן, ריטע וויַינשטיין, עליע מאַטיע באָקשטיין, וויכנע באָקשטיין, לייזער אַבראַמאָוויטש.
עס קניט: וואָווע וויַינשטיין

Photograph: In Dzierżoniów, from the right: Nyome Kagan, Rita Weinstein, Elye Motye Bokstein, Vichne Bokstein, Leizer Abramowicz. Kneeling: Vove Weinstein

We met acquaintances and good friends here. The teacher, Chava Segal, was the director of a Jewish children's boarding school, supported by the "Joint." Lonesome children found a warm home here. There, I met Pola, a former student of the Yiddish gymnasium in Bialystok. My acquaintance, Sarake Levitt and her parents, arrived here from Samarkand. It looked like life was beginning to stabilize.

Suddenly, during a calm evening, two brothers, butchers, were murdered in their butcher shop, while preparing the meat to be sold the following morning. Both of them had survived the death camps. One of them had not long before that, gotten married. A few weeks earlier we were at his wedding, and now – at the funeral. The mood among the Jewish crowd was terrible.

A short time later – another funeral. Young people from a kibbutz, which had been established here (I believe, from "Gordonia") were murdered. This strengthened the embitterment of the Jews against the Poles and Poland. We saw only one way out: to leave this bloody soil as quickly as possible. Groups of youths assembled themselves with the goal – to go to Israel. From Israel, emissaries arrived, who recruited the youths and aided them in fleeing Poland.

One's heart hurt from the losses of close and dear ones, already since the time when the Nazis looked forward to their rotten end, and it seemed that we, the bunch of saved Jews, could already benefit from some rest. A lot of people decided to emigrate as soon as possible to America, Canada, France, or make Aliyah to Israel. One stole across the border in the dark of night, taking with one small package and some dollars. Once again, one left behind, ownerless, one's new bit of belongings, which one had made one's own property. There was also a small legal immigration: the Polish powers that be gave out a limited number of transit permits.

We, too, presented a request to leave for Israel.

We were afraid to leave in a precarious manner because I was expecting a child.

In the meantime, my parents and my brother, Leizer, arrived. They had wanted to return "home" to Bereza. But after my father had seen the destruction of the town, they no longer had anything to look for there.

We had written to my parents that they should bring with them to Poland "piglets" and "noodles," that is, gold coins and dollars. They understood this literally, and indeed, brought with them packages of pig fat (shpek) and macaroni... They moved in with us. It was tight, but pleasant to be together: father and mother, a son, a daughter and her husband, and a grandchild on the way. There were few such families following our terrifying Holocaust.

A lot of homeless Jews moved into our city. In the streets, Jewish children appeared, for whom it was necessary to create an opportunity for study. In an old building of a former German school, a Jewish school of eight classes [grades] was established. The language of instruction was Yiddish. At the Jewish Committee it became known that I knew Yiddish, had studied the language. I was not looking for any work, although I already had a higher education and a certified specialization. They recommended that I give several lessons at the Jewish school, which was located a total of several hundred meters from our home. The school administration wanted to divide a large class of over 70 children into two classes: one class would be taken over by the old teacher, Josif Federbusz,[62] and I would take over the other class.

---

[62] The name of this and other Jewish teachers in postwar Dzierżoniów may be viewed at the following link: https://sztetl.org.pl/pl/miejscowosci/d/212-dzierzoniow/107-listy-nazwisk/83538-spis-nauczycieli-zamieszkalych-w-dzierzoniowie-maj-1946-r. In addition, a photo of Federbusz facing one of his students (c. 1955) may be seen at the following link: https://sztetl.org.pl/pl/media/103096-dzierzoniow-panstwowa-szkola-zydowska-nr-5 (accessed 3-4-24).

לערערס און געזעלשאַפטלעכע טוערס פון דער ייִדישער שול אין
דזשערדזשאָניוו. די אויטאָרין זיצט צווייטע פון רעכטס

Photograph: Teachers and social activists from the Jewish school in Dzierżoniów. The authoress is sitting second from the right.

And so, the students became rebellious. Everyone wanted to study with the other teacher. I entered a nearly empty class. Gradually, they grew accustomed to the thought that a young teacher would teach them. Most of the children did not have any common language; they spoke various tongues, and their Yiddish limped along very much. The children came from hiding places and holes, from the woods, from camps and monasteries, where they posed as Christians, spoke Polish, and did not remember any Yiddish. Also, a portion of the children were from the Soviet Union. They spoke Russian. So, I decided to tutor all of them in Yiddish following the classes. I did not tell anyone about this, so as to avoid any formalities, which could have created problems for me there. I also did not ask anyone that I be paid for this extra work.

In due time, the children became tied to me and even lovingly received their "young female teacher." When I had my birth vacation [i.e., maternity leave], their delegation came to me and asked that I return to school, as quickly as possible. They wrote down their request on a bar of chocolate, which they had brought me.

I interrupted my vacation a month early, so that the students could complete the school year as it needed to be done.

I Become a Mother

It was the end of February 1947. I came home from school and slipped on the ice, fell on the snow, stood up, shook the snow from myself, and moved on. When I related this to my mother, she gave me a strange look, because I was just about to give birth.

And this, indeed, is how it happened. We were sitting in the evening at the table, eating tasty sausage, and playing cards. Suddenly, I felt pains. When they began to come very frequently, my mother said that we must go to the hospital. We set out on foot, quite a distance. My husband and my father held me under the arms, so that I should not, heaven forbid, slip again. It did not occur to them that one could call an ambulance or a taxi.

A black, cold night. In the hospital there was not a single doctor. A nurse took me into the birthing room, and when I started to hemorrhage during the birth, she placed dirty snow on me from beneath the window...

I was fortunate: I endured, and in addition, had a son! My beautiful, thriving fellow brought me much joy. In the morning, the joy disappeared. I felt bad. They measured my temperature – 41 degrees [Celsius]. I threw up my entire dinner with the tasty sausage – it did not help. Nearly three weeks I was laid-up with a high fever. In the end, the examinations showed malaria, about which I had already entirely forgotten that past year.

I was seriously ill; I could not recognize people and saw them as though through a fog. My parents and my husband sat beside my bed, day, and night.

My husband knew about the new healing means of penicillin, for which one bartered on the black market. And so, he told the doctor that perhaps this medication could help me. So, they decided to try. A nurse watched over me the entire night, and every couple of hours, gave me injections of penicillin. And see and wonder – in the morning, the fever had fallen.

Until this day, I wear the jewelry that my husband gave me on the occasion of Shloymele's birth – a bracelet and a medallion.

At the same time, two more teachers from the Jewish school, Strykowksi and Halbersztadt, gave birth to boys. And so, for all three, we called upon a mohel.

At home, by us, we prepared ourselves for the delayed Brit-Milah. Our relatives, Hela and Bolek Sherf, prepared the refreshments. Aside from the family, friends and acquaintances assembled. It was pleasant sitting at the table in an exalted mood. Our firstborn we gave the name Shloyme for my husband's father.

After the bris, my child cried without end, and would not allow us to sleep at night. Blotches appeared on his tummy. We did not know the reason. Perhaps a bedbug had caused him this discomfort. We all suffered from this very affliction because it was an old, forlorn house.

Our friend, the agronomist, Avraham Goldstein, left for Warsaw and gave us his residence, along with the furniture. Previously, there had been a wealthy German domestic industry there – with pigs, cows, and fields to work. My mother learned how to milk the cows, and my father took up "agronomy" – planted the fields with whatever he could, particularly, with vegetables. Several Jewish families would buy fresh milk from us. In the house's attic I once found a tallit and several other things, which the German, it appears, stole from Jews.

The agronomists Halpern and Blum continued to reside in the same yard, and along with my parents, saw to the home economics. Halpern died suddenly at thirty-something years of age. His wife remained with two little young daughters; they would play in the garden with Shloymele. Mrs. Halpern began working at the school as a teacher of natural science.

My brother, Leizerke, became one of my students. For the eighth grade, I taught him chemistry and Yiddish. In the same class learned Heniek Nowarski, later an officer of Israel's merchant fleet, and the now well-known Israeli actress and singer, Lea Szlanger.[63]

My husband left for Wroclaw [Pol. Wrocław; formerly Breslau, Germany] and registered at the university to complete his studies in economics. He would come home only for Shabbat and Sunday.

We lived together with my parents, and they helped me raise my child and tend to the household duties. My brother, Leizerke, studied electronics at the established "ORT"[64] school. Although our life flowed normally and there were a lot of Jews around us, we indeed felt ourselves to be foreigners in the surrounding environment. We once again submitted a request to leave for Israel. However, they still refused us.

---

[63] Lea Szlanger (1932-1923) was a Polish-Jewish Israeli singer, actress, broadcaster, journalist, and translator. For further biographical details about her, see the following: https://forward.com/yiddish/539021/the-yiddish-actress-and-broadcaster-lea-szlanger-has-died-at-91/ (accessed 6-22-24).

[64] For further information about ORT and its history of vocational training, see: https://yivoencyclopedia.org/article.aspx/ORT (accessed 6-22-24).

1949 ,ייִדישע סטודענטן אין װראָצלאַװ

Photograph: Jewish students in Wroclaw, 1949

In the meantime, a year passed. Summertime, the Jewish families with little children left for the surrounding villages, to be in the country. We also rented a room from Polish peasants who had appropriated a villa and the fields of Germans who had fled. I recall the interesting book, which I read at that time – "Gone with the Wind." By us, too, everything was gone with the wind...

My husband decided to go see his hometown of Ciechanów and learn the details regarding the fate of his own. I went with him. Their home remained intact. In it, resided Poles. On the beds slept unfamiliar people. At the table from once-upon-a-time and the plates from once-upon-a-time ate strangers... And this was the same in all the Jewish houses. Not a single word of Yiddish was heard in the town. One single Jew now lived here. From my husband's parents, sisters and brothers, nobody remained. This was a distinguished family of grain dealers. His father had been an active Mizrachi-Zionist in the Jewish community. Until today, the surviving *landsleit* refer to him with respect.

The sum total was sorrowfully clear. We sold the house and the granaries dirt cheap, and with a grieving heart, said farewell to the hometown for good.

Jews, hailing from our hometowns – Ciechanów and Bereza – learned of us and came to visit us. We rejoiced, one with the other, as though we were the nearest relations. No genuine family relations actually remained... This is how Vove and Rita came to us for a few months before they left for Canada following a request from their relatives. It was very tight for us – three families in two rooms. We relinquished our own beds to our guests, but nobody complained.

Leizer Abramowicz,[65] a tall, handsome man from the village of Sporevo, also located us. During the war, he had been a commander of a partisan detachment in the Polesian woods. We all rejoiced upon his arrival, and recalled his house, to which, following the outbreak of the war, in September 1939, we had fled. My mother fried up potato pancakes for him – to recall former times and his home of once-upon-a-time. Leizer was now a Communist and had taken up an especially important post among the Poles. He also found work for my husband – a director position at a small paper factory. A few years later he got married to Dr. Bazierowa and had two beautiful daughters. He was the Polish Consul to the United States, China, and Turkey. From America, he would send food packages to my parents in Israel during the difficult period of economic austerity.

---

[65] Assuming the Leizer Abramowicz noted at the following webpage link is the same one by this name in the above text, he lived from 1909-2003 and is buried in the Warsaw Jewish Cemetery. See: https://www.geni.com/people/Leon-aleichemICZ/6000000004293375025 (accessed 6-22-24).

I would like to mention other good friends from Bereza, whom we encountered in Poland.

We always retained friendly relations with Nyome Kagan. He would even take risks and hide dollars in his home, which my husband was afraid to keep in our home.

Chava Segal was a teacher in the Bereza Yiddish school. She also worked in the Jewish school in Dzierżoniów as a teacher. The beautiful children's performances, which she would oversee, were extraordinarily successful. We enjoyed hearing her beautiful voice singing the heartfelt Yiddish songs of once-upon-a-time.

I visited with Chava and Vove twenty-something years later in Montreal, at Sonia and Leib Tencer's[66] home.

Rita, Vove's wife, unfortunately, was already gone by that time. Rita – a pretty girl from Bereza, from the few Jewish female students in the town, visited Vove in Tashkent. They got married and raised their family in Montreal, Canada.

Rita completed her studies here and received her MA. She died of a difficult illness. Both of her and Vove's sons completed their studies and left home. Vove remained alone. He and the Tencers received me very nicely, seeing to everything, so that I would have a pleasant visit in Canada.

Sonia, Leibel Tencer's wife, had survived the Vilna Ghetto and German concentration camps. When she arrived in Dzierżoniów, my mother helped her get settled into a room by us, in the yard.

---

[66] Additional biographical details about Leib Tencer (1910-) may be found at the following link: https://jplarchives.org/leib-tencer-fonds (accessed 6-22-24).

Sonia aspired to tear herself out of Poland, to her parents and husband, who were outside of the country. She tried to steal across the border with a group of Jews. The attempt fell through. They arrested her. The few dollars she had on her, she flushed down with water, in the toilet. She sat three months in prison. I had pity on the refined, pale, exhausted young woman. I once relinquished my bed to her, so that she might warm up her limbs, although I myself had a fever. Frozen and tired, she stood on her feet an entire night in the wagon, when she returned, disappointed, from Warsaw, having yet again received a refusal to her request to leave Poland legally. Sometime later, she nonetheless left. She united with her husband, Leib Tencer, and they left for Canada. Now they have two married daughters and grandchildren. Leib Tencer is a professor of Yiddish at the University of Montreal [i.e., McGill University].

It was a deep experience to meet with my old, good friends, and comrades. Recalling our youth, the common past, and singing the beloved Yiddish songs from once-upon-a-time.

In Poland we met with Chilek – Yechiel, our friend from the Samarkand institute. He was once again studying, along with my husband, at the University of Wroclaw, and together, they prepared for their diploma exams. Yechiel's big plans to become a prominent jewelry merchant ran amuck. Already at the end of his studies, he left Poland illegally via Czechoslovakia, so as to reach Israel and fight for the Jewish homeland – the Land of Israel.

Yechiel has been a dear friend of ours already ten score years. He is in general, a genuine friend of humanity and duly earns this very epithet.

My husband completed his studies, received a good position in the big city of Wroclaw, and we decided to relocate there.

My parents and my brother remained in Dzierżoniów, but not for long.

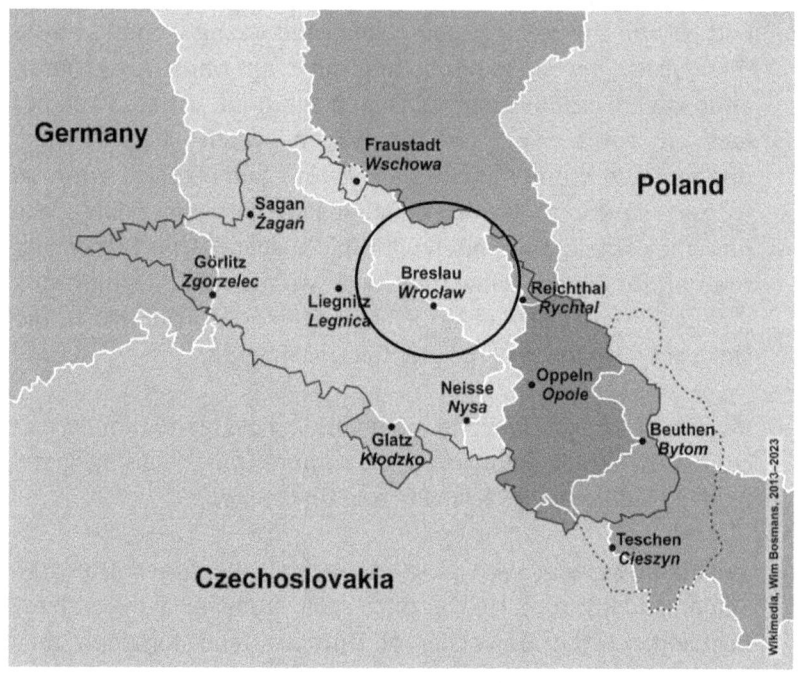

Map of Silesia in modern day Poland with Wroclaw (Breslau) as the focal point from FamilySearch's "Silesia (Schlesien), Prussia, German Empire Genealogy" webpage[67]

---

[67] See:
https://www.familysearch.org/en/wiki/Silesia_%28Schlesien%29,_Prussia,_German_Empire_Genealogy (accessed 6-25-24).

In Wroclaw

In Wroclaw we purchased the residence of Professor Stein, which he alone had renovated after the house had been damaged during the war. I had never before lived in such a beautiful apartment: four rooms with parquet floors, large windows, and balconies. Shloymele rode around on his little bicycle across the large hall. A bathroom was a completely new thing for us. In the bedroom stood furniture of mahogany wood, in the dining room – of walnut wood; on the walls – several original pictures; on the ceilings – beautiful lamps, candelabras. We also purchased for ourselves a service of beautiful porcelain, silver spoons, forks, and knives, new bedding, and towels.

All at once I had become a homemaker – oversaw the household duties, went shopping, and cooked. It was exceedingly difficult to go shopping for food products. One would stand for hours at a time in the store lines. Meat we would receive from a Polish woman who would bring it to our home, and she would take the price from the black market.

In the morning, I would go to the train station to await the peasants, who would come with baskets to the city to sell their products: eggs, butter – rolled up in green pages [or leaves], cheese in white linen sacks, and various fruits and vegetables. I would buy from them whatever was available because one could not attain these very products in the stores for government prices. While purchasing the living chickens, one had to, like once-upon-a-time, blow between the feathers to see whether they were fat. Charlotte, a German woman, would come twice a week to help with the housework. She told me that following a bombing of the city, she was buried beneath the ruins of their house, and they had barely schlepped her out from there.

And thus, we had full [or satisfying] years. I became busy with my child and with the house and stopped working. There was plenty to live on. My husband, as an economist with a diploma, worked for a large trade enterprise and earned well.

Opposite our house was a square – a garden with trees and benches. I would go there with the baby carriage, and sitting on a bench, would read books in Polish, Russian, and Yiddish. Other Jewish mothers would also come here with their young ones, and I developed an acquaintanceship with several of them. While our children were playing in the sand, one would relate to the other one's own experiences. And everyone had something to relate...

None of the Jewish children spoke Yiddish. I tried to raise my child with Yiddish. It, however, did not work. He would create sentences that were half-Polish, half-Yiddish.

My brother, Leizer, came to Wroclaw for an exhibition of his "ORT" school to exhibit an electronic apparatus, which the students had constructed. And so, he stayed with us for several months as a good, desirable guest.

Around us, we had many good friends and comrades. In particular, we befriended Dr. Jużek Makowski[68] and his wife, Wanda. We would come to them for the Polish Easter and bring a box of matzos, which Wanda, the Pole [i.e., Gentile Polish woman] really loved. She would prepare a broiled rabbit and other Polish delicacies. We would invite them to our Passover Seder, with matzoh balls, gefilte fish, and other dishes. The four glasses of wine, it is understood, were not lacking...

Before the war, Jużek had taught in Mlawa [Mława], in the Polish-Jewish gymnasium, together with my husband. Jużek had a fantastic biography. During the Nazi occupation, he and a

---

[68] Jużek is a nickname for Józef [Makowski] (1909-1992). See: https://search.worldcat.org/title/2951959 (6-24-24).

comrade had succeeded in fleeing from the death camp, Majdanek. Later on, he posed as a German and served in the German military. He is blonde, has blue eyes, knows perfect German, and speaks without an accent. And so, he succeeded in fooling the Germans; and, just so as to anger Hitler, remained alive.

He described his experiences in the book, "Wehrmachtgefolge,"[69] which was translated into several languages. I read over that book in a single breath one sleepless night. The family of Dr. Makowski later left for Denmark, where they reside until today.

We also sustained a friendship with Sarkale Levitt, the Samarkand student, who thereafter, in Poland, completed her studies in medicine. She became our home doctor. She was pretty, refined, and pleasant-natured. With her husband, Leon Herzog, she left for London. He – for a high-ranking Polish government post. In his honor, she merited, along with the other diplomats, to be present at the coronation of the Queen of England. Her parents were active Communists.

In Wroclaw, I used to like coming to the Levitts, along with Shloymele, for a glass of tea and the small, unusually tasty cookies that Sarkale's mother would bake, and treat guests to, always smiling. Today, the Herzog family resides in Sweden. They fled from Poland with the stream of Jewish refugees during the Six Day War, when an ugly government anti-Semitism raged there. Sarkale's parents died in Sweden. The Herzogs visit us from time to time.

---

[69] The bibliographic details of this publication (in the original Polish) are as follows: Józef Makowski, *Wehrmachtgefolge* (Warsaw: Czytelnik, 1962).

It was very pleasant visiting Musye and Boris Sadovnik. Him I knew from earlier on. Musye's parents lived here together with them and ran a beautiful Jewish household. It was said that her mother was a beauty and that her father had done time in the Kartuz-Bereza concentration camp for Communism. On the birthday of Musye and Boris' daughters, many comrades and *landsleit* from the town of Dubna, from which the family hailed, came together. On the tables were all sorts of goodies. We enjoyed the tasty foods and also had a nice time. At the table, everyone, together, sang Yiddish, Russian, and Polish songs.

At the Sadovniks I met Ada and Siome Roginski, the pharmacist, and Niura and Grisha Inspektor, the chemical engineer. Regarding Niura, it was related that during the Nazi occupation, she hid under a bridge. In her hair, she would weave in clean white ribbons, so that people would think that she had a home… However, she was caught and brought into the Gestapo. The German, in whose domain she had fallen, hid her in a cabinet, and at night, allowed her to run away.

Up until today, I am [still] friendly with all these good friends and comrades from that time.

Summertime, we would mostly leave Wroclaw for the Baltic Sea and greatly enjoy ourselves on the pristine, light sand of the local beaches, enjoying the cool sea water. We could hide our shoes from the baking sun in the large, straw baskets deployed on the shore. In the evenings we would go out dancing at the nightclubs. In short, we lived it up!

Shloymele would cause me much grief with his frequent colds and the angina from which he suffered. In addition, a white blister broke out on his penis. I became frightened: perhaps he had contracted a venereal disease on the beach… Or, he had contracted something when he had gone out to the sea in the middle of the night looking for me, when the landlady did not hear this. A three-year-old boy alone on the seashore at night... I had enough fright. So, I promised myself not to go out and to have a good time until late.

Once, Shloymele began hitting a Polish child who had insulted him by calling him a "Żyd."

My husband would come to us only for a short time. The work kept him tied down. Also here, at the sea, he met comrades from home – Irke and Tewek Ruda. Great was the joy of the encounter following the difficult war years. Tewek and Irke – a nice couple, both with high-up government posts in Poland. They were both here to relax with their two daughters. While still in their youth, my husband had introduced both of them, and it became a match. We are friends for ten score years. *Landsleit*, comrades from youth – this is like a familial relationship following our major catastrophe [Holocaust], when one remained without one's one and nearest.

Our comrades, Marysia and Michał Haller, former students of the University of Wroclaw, and also Bronka and her father and brother, the officer of the Polish Army, lived in villas at the edge of the city. Going to them, we saw how Wroclaw had suffered from the effects of war. Terrible traces of the war – houses that had been broken into pieces, ruins of complete quarters, wild, overgrown gardens, and thoroughly singed trees. Slowly, the city council restored ruined places, such as the "rynek,"[70] where they built new houses according to the old models.

Many newcomer residents – Polish and Jewish families, settled in the large, ruined city of Wroclaw.

---

[70] "Rynek" is Polish for "market" or "marketplace." Many cities and towns throughout Poland have at their center, a "rynek."

There was a large shortage of apartments. And this forced a person to have an area of residence that was limited up to eight square meters. We had a large apartment and needed to downsize. So, we took in sub-tenants, so that they would leave us alone and not send in someone just for the sake of it. In the largest room with the Venetian window, which stood empty, moved in a woman with her son, a student – Maria and Ryszek Szalejski. We lived nicely with them. Both of them were blonde with blue eyes and could pass for Poles. Their "Aryan" appearance indeed helped them to hide in Warsaw, after they had succeeded at the last minute to flee from the ghetto trap.

The other female neighbor, Halina Schicker, had divorced her husband in Lodz, and we took her in to [live with] us. She would work in the house – painting various wooden and ceramic products. She would help me prepare the food and baked goods for Shloymele's birthday, or for when we had invited over guests. We would have a good time at the covered table, sing hearty Russian war songs, Yiddish, and Polish folksongs, former "hits," relate comical and tragic experiences, which was not lacking by any one of us.

When my second son, Bebuś [pronounced Bebush; a Polish diminutive] was born, the three sub-tenants had to leave the residence. Maria Szalejski gave me a present – books with directions for cooking and baking. On them she wrote a dedication: "As a memento for the dear mother of my beloved grandchild, Shloymele." She and her son left for their relatives in France.

Halina Schicker had no choice and returned to her husband. She married him anew. Shloymele liked her a lot and gave her flowers at her departure.

In Wroclaw we led a normal and good life. We frequently went to the opera, which stood on a high artistic level. We greatly enjoyed the shows, which the Yiddish government theater named for Esther-Rochel Kaminska, in Warsaw, would bring down to us. The theater performed by us in a building that had been specially designated for it. The performances, "Mirele Efros" and "Meir Ezofowicz," with Ida Kaminska at the head of her good ensemble,[71] are inscribed in my memory.

We would also attend the lectures and cultural activities, which the Yiddish Culture Association [YKUF] in Poland carried out in Wroclaw. And in this manner, we sustained our spiritual [or intellectual] connection to Yiddish literature, art, and culture.

My husband, as I already said, worked for a trade enterprise, and in addition – in an office for energy. Having stable help for the household tasks and with the children, I also went to go work in my specialization – as a licensed expert in textiles and in the leather industry for a large firm of imported materials – "Galluks."

Our second son, Berele (named for my brother) – we called him Bebuś, for short, was born a lovely dark little fellow, with long, curly hair, like a Yemenite. In the hospital where I gave birth to him worked our good friend, Dr. Boris Sadovnik, and he was the first one to see my newborn, and delivered good greetings to me from him...

At first, Bebuś would cry entire nights, and I, not having slept, would go around by day, like a drunk. My help, Nellie, an eighteen-year-old Gentile girl with blonde braids and beautiful light eyes, tended to him.

---

[71] For additional information about the post-World War II Yiddish theater in Warsaw and performers, Esther-Rochel Kaminska (1870-1925) and her daughter, Ida Kaminska (1899-1980), see: https://www.teatr-zydowski.art.pl/en/about-us/history (accessed 4-13-24).

די אויטאָרין מיטן מאַן און זון שלמהלע

Photograph: the authoress with her husband and son, Shloymele

She would also stay overnight by us. I think that my husband really liked her. In the morning, when he would go into the room to wake her, it would take a bit too long... I did not want to send him packing "due to a moment's anger,"[72] and swallowed my jealousy. I did not want to become the laughingstock of anyone. I decided to lead a calm life, without scandals. And I never brought up any discussion about this subject.

The second help was already older and ugly. She became strongly connected to the children and would say in front of everyone

---

[72] This approximates the original Yiddish expression, which essentially connotes that the author did not want to take any overly hasty actions, due to the heat of the moment, or as the result of simple jealousy.

that these were her sons. From her salary she would buy them toys, go with them to the zoological garden, and go to children's performances.

There was a great improvement felt in the life of the residents in the Polish cities on former German territory. But for Jews... The anti-Semitism could be felt at every step. There were instances when a Jew would speak Yiddish on the train and get beaten up by Polish hooligans.

With our Polish neighbors in the house, we had no contact. We were increasingly convinced that this was not our place, although materially, we were not lacking for anything, and lived, as with once-upon-a-time, in prosperity.

For Israel!

We knew that our existence in Poland must come to an end. So, we bombarded the Polish government agencies with letters, so that they would allow us to leave for Israel, to go to my parents and brother who had gone there in 1950. However, they would constantly refuse us. Perhaps, because at that time in Poland, there were still not enough academic cadres, and so they would not allow Jews with higher education to leave.

Only at the end of 1956, when Gomułka once again came to power,[73] did we suddenly receive permission to immigrate to Israel. Our joy was great on account of this good news, although we knew from the letters from my family that the situation in Israel was difficult, both politically and economically, and that they barely earned a living, while we were living very well – easily and fulfilled...

And not only did we live easily and fulfilled in Poland, then. Many Jews – in high-up government positions, played a big role in the ruling Communist Party, in literature, and in art, in the press, in industry, and in commerce. And they did not want to leave Poland, where they had acclimated, and built homes and families in the new environment. Nonetheless, we felt that Jews envied us, the first two families – us and the Okienskis – who were leaving Poland legally. After years of waiting, we left to unite with our nearest.

Hundreds of Jews accompanied us in Wroclaw to the train station. People said goodbye to us with tears in their eyes and wished us all the best.

---

[73] For further context about Gomułka's leadership of Poland between the years 1956 to 1970, see for instance:
https://www.britannica.com/biography/Wladyslaw-Gomulka (accessed 4-13-24).

Before leaving Wroclaw we sold the apartment and furniture. And at this point there began a mad rush to the stores to purchase goods in exchange for money, since we were not permitted to take any currency with us, and Polish zlotys had no value outside of Poland. And so, we bought an accordion, rugs, various utensils, an ice box, a radio and a stereo, crystal, silver, a camera, down covers, and jewelry. We packed everything in large boxes and sent it by sea to Israel. The packages with bedding were bound up in thick twine, inside of which, our good friend hid the last bit of dollars.

We also said our cordial goodbyes to the Polish neighbors from across the way and gave them various household goods. The Poles were, indeed, glad that the Jews were leaving Poland. Once, their slogan had indeed been: "Jews – to Palestine!"

Acquaintances came to ask us what was worthwhile to bring to Israel. It was clear that they, too, were toying with the idea of leaving Poland, so as to unite with the large Jewish family – with the Jewish people in its historical homeland. The Jewish emigration from Poland began anew, then, and we were among the first to merit this.

For understandable reasons, few Jews in Poland openly declared themselves Zionists, but the reality was that the anti-Semitic surroundings, the shudders experienced from the Second World War, did what was good for ourselves: we strengthened our national consciousness and the conclusion that as long as we were destined to live, it must be in our own home, in an environment of Jews as free citizens of our own country, where we could hand down to our children's children that which our generation had lived through, and the conclusion that we must deduce from that.

די אויטאָרין מיט אירעביידע זין שלמהלע און בעבוש

Photograph: the authoress with both of her sons, Shloymele and Bebuś

די משפחה אין ישראל.
פון רעכטס: דער מאַן, דער זון שלמהלע, די מאַמע פון דער אויטאָרין, די אויטאָרין, איר פֿאָטער, איר ברודער לייזער; אין מיטן: דער זון בעבוש

Photograph: The family in Israel. From the right: my husband, my son, Shloymele, the mother of the authoress, the authoress, her father, [and] her brother, Leizer; in the middle: her son, Bebuś.

From Wroclaw we went to Warsaw, where we had to take care of several more formalities prior to leaving Poland. In Warsaw, our dear friends, the parents of Sarkele Herzog-Levitt, gave us their dwelling for the two days that we were in the city. Jużek Makowski cordially accompanied our little family to the train.

With much hope and also, some heart thumping, we once again took our wandering staff in hand. Without any regret; on the contrary, with true joy, we left behind the Polish soil, which is thoroughly saturated with Jewish blood and Jewish tears...

The First Part of My Life

מ. בערנשטיין: צייכענונג

Drawing: M. Bernstein

INDEX

A

Abramowicz, Leizer, 66, 142, 150, 159
Aleichem, Sholem, 36, 43, 47, 48
Alexandrovsky, Chaim, 41
Alexandrovsky, Chaimke, 37
America, 20, 27, 58, 64, 141, 143, 147, 151, 159
Aminov, Dr., 95, 98, 99, 116
Anders, General, 121
Argentina, 26, 141
Arian, Dr., 65, 66
Arian, Mrs., 31
Arian, Witek, 65
Arontshik, 117, 129, 130
Asch, Shalom, 36, 46
Ashgabat, 119, 134
Auschwitz, 75, 127
Australia, 63, 64, 76, 147
Avrahamel (student), 117

B

Babitsh family, 52, 55, 57
Babitsh, Yosl, 75, 142
Bandera, Stepan Andriyovych, 70
Barbel (teacher), 75
Bazierowa, Dr., 159
Bebuś (Fannie's son), 168, 169, 174, 175
Benny (Fannie's son), 139
Berele (Fannie's brother), 29
Berele (Fannie's son), 169

Bereza, 3, 8, 12, 17, 20, 23, 24, 34, 35, 37, 46, 49, 52, 54, 56, 59, 60, 62, 67, 68, 70, 72, 73, 74, 75, 76, 77, 78, 79, 81, 82, 83, 85, 86, 91, 98, 101, 107, 127, 130, 132, 134, 135, 136, 138, 139, 140, 141, 142, 151, 159, 160
Bereza Ghetto, 61, 73
Bereza Kartuska, 6, 18, 138
Bereza-Kartuska, 8, 13, 14, 17
Berkovitch, Danye, 50
Berkovitch, Leikele, 73
Berman (teacher), 48
Bernstein, M., 137, 177
Bernstein, Mordechai V., 141
Bernstein, Moyshele, 23, 40, 74, 143
Bessarabia, 21
Bialystok, 3, 52, 53, 54, 55, 59, 60, 61, 63, 64, 65, 68, 103, 150
Bialystok Ghetto, 62, 63, 64
Biletzky, Y. Ch., 11, 12
Biltshik, Chana, 35
Biltshik, Yossel, 49
Bludnye, 20, 54, 68, 138
Blum (agronomist), 156
Blumenfeld, Diana, 46
Bobruisk, 82
Bokstein, Berele, 23, 57, 80, 91, 92, 94, 99, 102, 106, 107, 108, 117, 124, 139
Bokstein, Elye Motye, 150

Bokstein, Elye-Motye, 29, 49
Bokstein, Leizer, 80, 139, 151, 164, 175
Bokstein, Leizerke, 87, 99, 107, 127, 128, 157
Bokstein, Vichne, 28, 29, 49, 107, 150
Boris (student), 128
Boyan (teacher), 30
Boyan, Leibel, 35, 49
Brazil, 65
Brenner family, 6, 7
Brisk, 27, 28, 55, 79
Brodsky, Nyunye, 56
Bronka, 167
Bronna-Góra, 136, 138
Broyde, Nyome, 51
Byaroza, 8

C

Canada, 4, 141, 147, 151, 159, 160, 161
Chelyabinsk, 100, 106, 107, 121, 127, 128, 135, 144
Chilek, 129, 130, 134, 161
Chilek (student), 116, 117
China, 143, 159
Chmiel, Rochel, 35
Chmiel-Shapiro, 49
Chmiel-Shapiro, Rochel, 31, 138
Chomsky, Dov, 142
Chorew (ice-cream seller), 40, 139
Ciankali, 138
Ciechanów, 158, 159

D

Denmark, 165
Derevyagin, Lieutenant, 73
Djuma, 111, 112
Dovid (Fannie's uncle), 27
Dubna, 166
Dzierżoniów, 148, 150, 152, 153, 160, 162

E

Epstein-Sklyar, Beba, 75
Eshman (photographer), 65
Estonia, 119

F

Faigel (Fannie's grandmother), 27
Federbusz, Josif, 152
Feld (teacher), 35, 36
France, 151, 168
Fredek (Fannie's husband), 117, 120, 121, 122, 124, 125, 126, 127, 129, 134, 144
Friedman, Moyshel, 48
Friedman, Moyshele, 49

G

Galia, 130, 133
Garber, Mulik, 44
Garber, Rochel, 49
Gdansk, 62
Gdynia, 62
Gebirtig, Mordechai, 45
Gelroth (teacher), 59

Germany, 6, 18, 24, 66, 72, 78, 79, 126, 146
Gershgorn, Malke, 37
Gilinsky, Chaimke, 56
Glaser family, 75, 76
Glaser, Chayekele, 75, 76
Glaser, Yisroelik, 76
Glaser, Yitzchak-Ezra, 75
Glogowski, Naomi, 62, 64
Glotserman, 83
Goberman, Itzel, 44, 65, 74
Goldberg, Chaya/Clara, 26, 27, 85, 101, 112, 125, 131
Goldberg, Dovid, 26, 27, 85, 101, 111, 125, 131
Goldberg, Fimke, 115, 116, 131
Goldberg, Siome, 130
Goldberg, Siomke, 116
Goldstein, Avraham, 156
Gomułka, 7, 172
Gorki, 46
Gorska, Halina, 62

H

Hadera, 128
Halbersztadt (teacher), 156
Haller, Marysia, 167
Haller, Michał, 167
Halpern family, 156
Halpern, Leikele, 44
Hamsun, 46
Heniek (student), 116, 120
Hershel (brother of Machlye), 52
Herzog family, 165
Herzog, Leon, 165
Herzog-Levitt, Sarkele, 175
Hirshfeld, Abrasha, 114
Hirszhorn, Dr., 147
Hitler, 68, 73, 121, 165
Holon, 140
Homel, 82
Hugo, Victor, 46

I

Inspektor, Grisha, 166
Inspektor, Niura, 166
Israel, 3, 4, 6, 7, 98, 113, 114, 139, 140, 141, 148, 149, 151, 157, 159, 161, 172, 173, 175

J

Janka (Fannie's friend), 120
Jedwab, Leike, 64

K

Kagan (shoemaker), 31
Kagan, Hershel, 49
Kagan, Nyome, 150, 160
Kagan, Shayme, 30
Kagan, Shilim, 49
Kamenetzky, 68
Kamenetzky, Shloyme, 49
Kaminska, Ida, 46, 169
Kaplan, Emma, 49
Kaplan, Leibel, 31, 35, 49
Kaplan, Michlye, 60, 61
Kaplan, Taibele, 41, 139
Karolitzky, Itzel, 37
Kartuz, 15, 139

Kartuz-Bereza, 7, 8, 10, 11, 17, 19, 20, 21, 24, 32, 65, 70, 131, 166
Kasierski sisters, 50
Kasierski, Leitshe, 139
Kataev, Valentin Petrovich, 87
Kazakhstan, 76
Kerensky, 46
Kielce, 145
Kiev, 102, 133
Kiryat-Shaul, 139
Kosava, 76, 77, 80, 81, 103
Koval, Moyshele, 49
Koval, Rivka, 49
Koval, Shaye, 49
Koval, Zindel, 49
Krakow, 45, 116
Kronik, Hershel, 49
Kuvanov, Juri, 14

L

Latvia, 119, 131
Leah (sister of Machlye), 55
Leizer (Fannie's uncle), 26, 27
Leizerke (Fannie's brother), 29
Lemberg, 3, 129, 130, 132, 133, 134, 135, 144
Leningrad, 3, 26, 80, 82, 84, 85, 86, 87, 88, 92, 101, 115, 117, 130, 131
Levin family, 56, 57, 59, 60
Levinson brothers, 79
Levinson, Mulik, 65
Levinson, Vovik, 40, 41, 42, 65, 79
Levitan, Yuri, 92, 126
Levitt family, 165

Levitt, Sarake, 150
Levitt, Sarkale, 165
Lithuania, 10, 21, 119
Liza (student), 120
Lodz, 146, 168
London, 165
Lower Silesia, 146, 148
Lozer (student), 72, 73
Lublin, 146, 147
Luck, 121
Lyube (Fannie's aunt), 86

M

Machlye (Fannie's friend), 31, 40, 52, 53, 54, 55, 56, 58, 60, 61
Majdanek, 165
Makiewka (ice-cream seller), 40
Makowski, Jużek, 164, 175
Makowski, Wanda, 164
Manger, Itsik, 59
Mark, Berl, 64
Markish, Peretz, 46
Marx, Karl, 110
Matinian, Professor, 104, 105
Michael (water carrier), 25
Michurinsk, 89
Mickiewicz, 46, 74
Mirele (Fannie's friend), 40
Mogilev, 82
Molodowsky, Kadya, 11, 141
Molotov, 79
Moniek, 130
Montreal, 160, 161
Morse, Stephen P., 13, 14

Moscow, 17, 83, 92, 105, 113, 132, 147
Moyshe (Fannie's uncle), 27

N

Nadya (maid), 32
Natasha (student), 120
Nellie, 169
New York, 76, 142
Novik, Moyshele, 49
Nowarski, Heniek, 157

O

Okienski family, 172
Opatoshu, 46
Orsha, 82
Orzeszkowa, 46
Osher, 119
Osher (student), 117
Osher, Reb, 23

P

Palestine, 135, 173
Paraguay, 65
Paris, 32, 54, 64
Penza, 92
Peretz, I. L., 36, 62
Philadelphia, 27
Pinek (student), 117
Pinsk, 65
Podostroytse, Leibel, 49
Pola (student), 150
Poland, 3, 6, 7, 10, 17, 21, 24, 36, 63, 66, 68, 72, 73, 78, 85, 98, 106, 108, 115, 116, 117, 120, 126, 127, 131, 133, 143, 144, 145, 146, 147, 151, 152, 160, 161, 162, 165, 167, 169, 172, 173, 175
Polesia, 138
Polishuk, Nellie, 102, 103
Pruzhany, 28, 75, 76, 103, 139, 141, 142
Pruzhany Ghetto, 142

R

Ratner family, 66
Reed, John, 46
Reichenbach, 148
Reisner family, 62
Reisner, Nechama, 62
Resnik family, 28, 50
Resnik, Moyshel, 65
Resnik, Sarale, 65
Resnik, Yoyne, 36
Reymont, 46
Riga, 131
Risker, Bayltshe, 49
Roginski, Ada, 166
Roginski, Siome, 166
Rolland, 46
Rtishchevo, 89
Rubina (Fannie's friend), 132
Ruda, Irke, 167
Ruda, Tewek, 167
Russia, 3, 29, 46, 58, 85, 87, 88, 119, 128

S

S., Yossel (student), 130
Sadovnik, Boris, 166, 169

Sadovnik, Musye, 166
Samarkand, 3, 10, 93, 94, 96, 97, 98, 100, 102, 103, 105, 107, 108, 109, 110, 112, 113, 115, 116, 117, 119, 120, 121, 122, 127, 128, 130, 132, 133, 150, 161, 165
Sapieha, Prince, 15
Sapir (barber), 30
Sara (merchant's daughter), 119
Sarale (student), 120
Schicker, Halina, 168
Segal, Chava, 35, 48, 49, 150, 160
Segalowitz, 46
Semyon, Michał, 67, 68, 71
Shaftan (teacher), 30
Shaftan, Eliyahu, 35, 36
Shaftan, Elye, 49
Shaftan, Gite, 35, 49
Shapiro, Chmiel, 49
Shapiro, Dinke, 43
Shereshev, 28, 141
Sherf, Bolek, 156
Sherf, Hela, 156
Shloymele (Fannie's son), 156, 157, 163, 165, 166, 167, 168, 170, 174, 175
Shtuker, Lozer, 65, 79
Shtuker-Paiuk, Masha, 142
Shulman, Ite, 56, 58, 64
Sienkiewicz, 46
Smolensk, 83, 85, 120
Sommerstein, Emil, 148
South Africa, 147
South America, 63, 65
Soviet Union, 72, 76, 78, 79, 81, 85, 87, 92, 98, 111, 113, 121, 132, 139, 145, 153
Spektor, Yitzchak-Elchanan, 142
Sporevo, 66, 159
Stalin, 105, 111
Stam, Itzel, 63
Stein, Professor, 163
Stola, Dariusz, 7
Stolpce, 80
Strykowksi (teacher), 156
Sweden, 165
Świdnica, 146, 148
Szalejski, Maria, 168
Szalejski, Ryszek, 168
Szlanger, Lea, 157

T

Tabalitzky, 22
Tagore, Rabindranath, 74
Tambov Oblast, 87, 90
Tashkent, 92, 93, 119, 127, 160
Tel-Aviv, 139, 142
Tencer, Leib, 160, 161
Tencer, Leibel, 160
Tencer, Sonia, 160
Tishler, Aron, 56
Tkatch, Eliyahu, 49
Tkatch, Nittel, 49
Tolstoy, 46
Tonye, 130, 133, 134
Tshesler, Baylke, 49
Tuchman, Moyshe, 138, 140
Turkey, 143, 159

Turkiewicz, Dr., 126
Turkow, Zygmunt, 46

U

Ukraine, 119, 135, 146
Uruguay, 65
Uzbekistan, 93, 97, 118, 130

V

Verne, Jules, 46
Vichne (Fannie's mother), 27
Vilna, 43, 52, 65, 72, 73
Vilna Ghetto, 160
Volodya (student), 113

W

Warsaw, 11, 17, 46, 52, 66, 106, 127, 142, 146, 147, 148, 156, 161, 168, 169, 175
Warsaw Ghetto, 126
Warsaw Jewish Cemetery, 159
Weinstein, Rita, 150, 159, 160
Weinstein, Shloyme, 35, 49
Weinstein, Shloymeke, 39
Weinstein, Shloymke, 49
Weinstein, Vove, 49, 127, 150, 159, 160
Weinstein, Zlata, 49
White Russia, 36, 67, 119, 146
Wiśniewski, Tomasz, 13
Wroclaw, 3, 157, 158, 161, 162, 163, 164, 165, 166, 167, 168, 169, 172, 173, 175

Y

Yaffe, Osher, 86
Yalom (teacher), 98, 99
Yalom, Emma, 91
Yalom, Leizer, 91, 101
Yalon, Chayetshe, 49
Yechezkel (student), 120
Yosef, 130
Yovarkovsky, Moyshe, 56
Yuri (engineer), 113

Z

Zackheim family, 79
Zackheim, Nyome, 65, 73
Zackheim, Yankel, 49
Zackheim, Zelik, 49
Zakopane, 72
Zalevsky, Meir-Yossel, 25, 27
Zelicki, Pawel, 148
Zhabinka, 76
Zshenia (student), 119

www.ingramcontent.com/pod-product-compliance
Lightning Source LLC
Chambersburg PA
CBHW071846230426

43671CB00012B/2082